OLE!

ED EMBERLEY'S BIG PURPLE DRAWING BOOK

LITTLE, BROWN AND COMPANY
BOSTON TORONTO

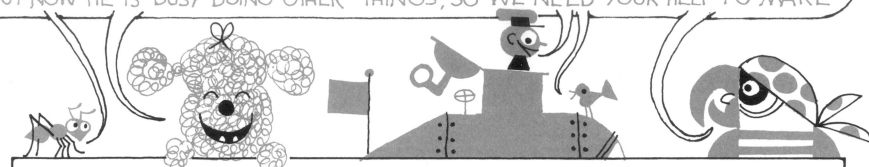

HELLO! WE ARE THE "PICTURE PEOPLE" ED EMBERLEY PUT US IN THIS BOOK, BUT NOW HE IS BUSY DOING OTHER THINGS, SO WE NEED YOUR HELP TO MAKE

HC: 10 9 8 7 6
★ PB: 10 9

LIBRARY OF CONGRESS CATALOGING IN PUBLICATION DATA

EMBERLEY, ED.
    ED EMBERLEY'S BIG PURPLE DRAWING BOOK.

    SUMMARY: PRESENTS STEP-BY-STEP INSTRUCTIONS FOR DRAWING PEOPLE, ANIMALS, AND OBJECTS USING A MINIMUM OF LINE AND CIRCLE COMBINATIONS.
    1. DRAWING--TECHNIQUE--JUVENILE LITERATURE.
2. PURPLE IN ART--JUVENILE LITERATURE. [1. DRAWING--TECHNIQUE]
I. TITLE. II. TITLE: BIG PURPLE DRAWING BOOK.

NC670.E46   741.2'6   81-3778
ISBN 0-316-23422-2   AACR2
ISBN 0-316-23423-0 (PBK.)

PUBLISHED SIMULTANEOUSLY IN CANADA BY LITTLE, BROWN AND COMPANY LTD. (CANADA)
PRINTED IN THE UNITED STATES OF AMERICA

US "LIVE". IF YOU WOULD TAKE US OUT ONCE IN A WHILE (BY DRAWING US) AND LET US DO THINGS WE WOULD BE MOST GRATEFUL!

CONTENTS

INSTRUCTIONS

| THIS ROW SHOWS WHAT TO DRAW. | THIS ROW SHOWS WHERE TO PUT IT. | | | | | |

THIS SIGN MEANS "FILL IN"

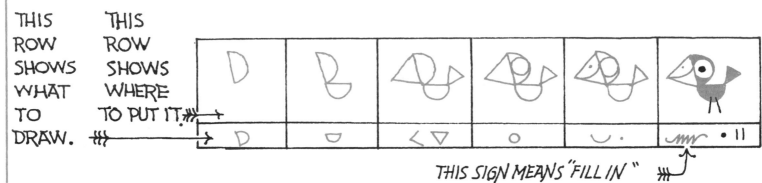

THIS ALPHABET WAS USED TO MAKE ALL THE WORDS IN THIS BOOK.
ABCDEFGHIJKLMNOPQRSTUVWXYZ

THIS ALPHABET WAS USED TO MAKE ALL THE PICTURES IN THIS BOOK.
(■●▼ ∨ ◗ ⊂ ╎.)

4

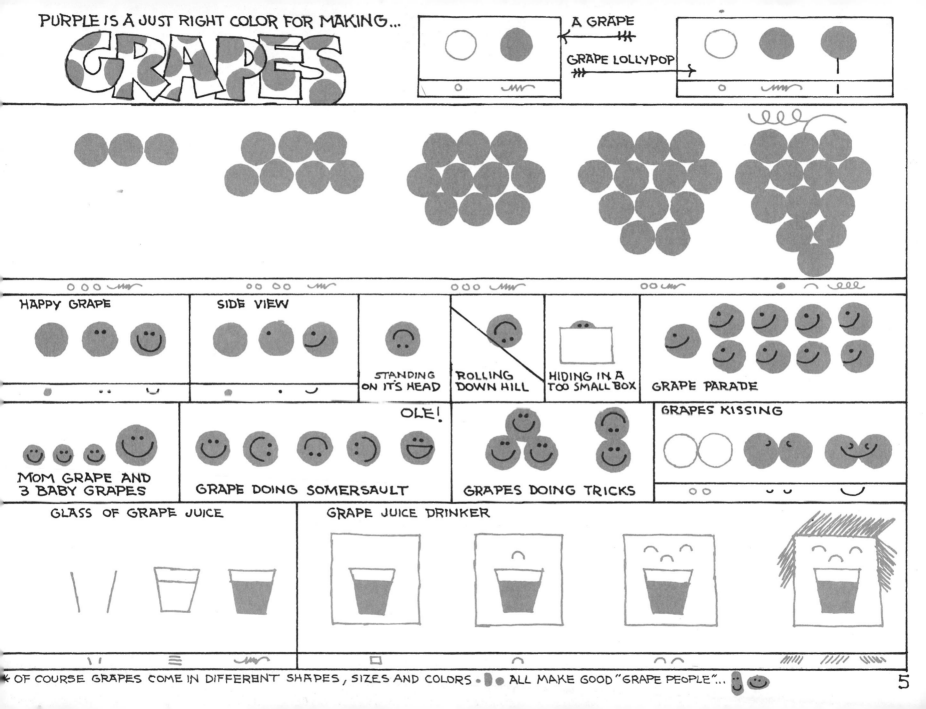

PURPLE IS A JUST RIGHT COLOR FOR MAKING...

GRAPES

A GRAPE

GRAPE LOLLYPOP

HAPPY GRAPE

SIDE VIEW

STANDING ON IT'S HEAD

ROLLING DOWN HILL

HIDING IN A TOO SMALL BOX

GRAPE PARADE

MOM GRAPE AND 3 BABY GRAPES

OLE!

GRAPE DOING SOMERSAULT

GRAPES DOING TRICKS

GRAPES KISSING

GLASS OF GRAPE JUICE

GRAPE JUICE DRINKER

⚓ OF COURSE GRAPES COME IN DIFFERENT SHAPES, SIZES AND COLORS ● ALL MAKE GOOD "GRAPE PEOPLE"...

THE NESSYS

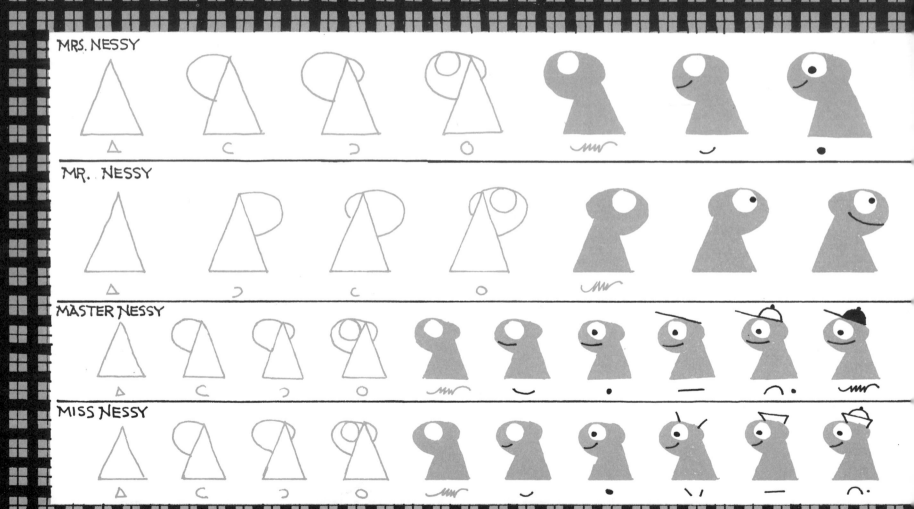

MRS. NESSY

MR. NESSY

MASTER NESSY

MISS NESSY

OTHER ASSORTED NESSYS

CAN YOU FIGURE OUT HOW I DREW THEM?

NESSY TAIL

NESSY BODY
(LOOK ABOVE TO SEE HOW 🌲 IT FITS.)

A NESSY PEEKING UP
OUT OF THE WATER

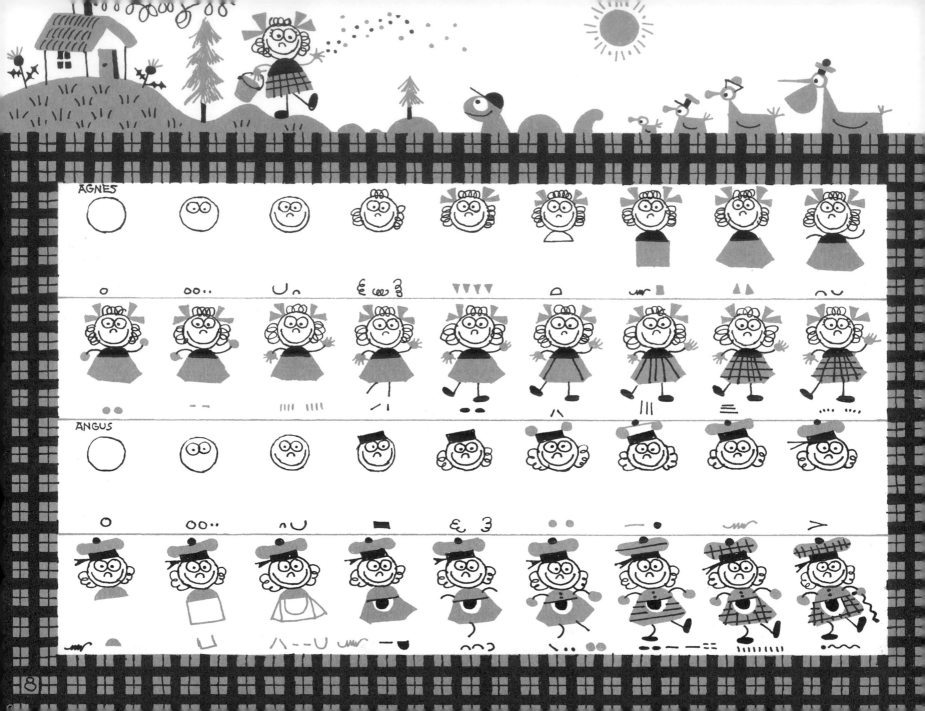

AGNES

ANGUS

PELICAN

DUCKS

ROCKS

WITH GRASS   WITH FLOWERS

NOTICE HOW THE SAME SIZE NESSY CAN BE MADE TO LOOK BIGGER OR SMALLER, DEPENDING ON WHAT YOU PUT NEXT TO IT.

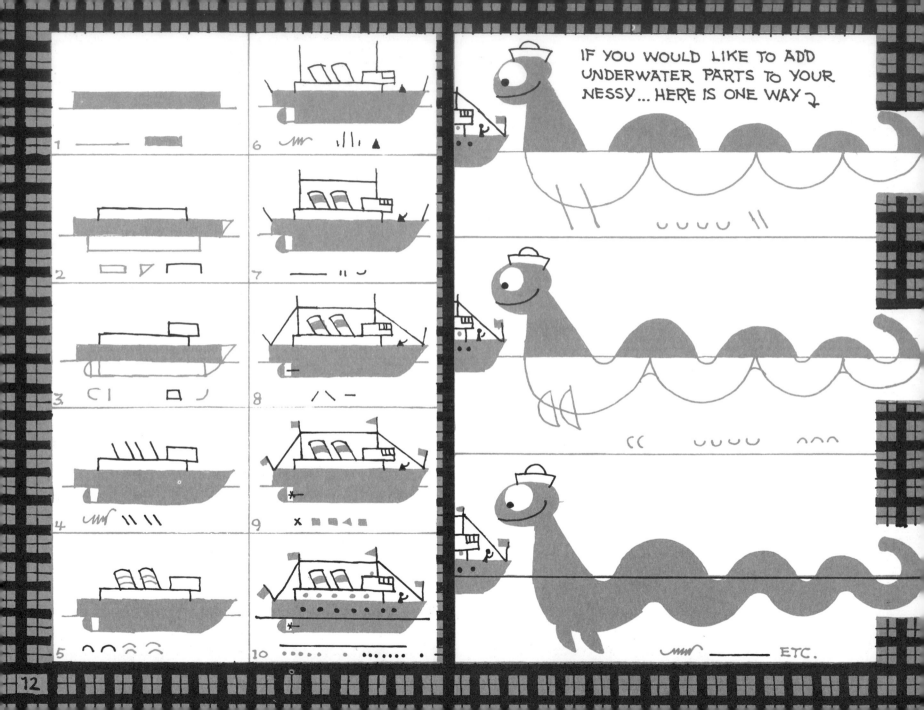

IF YOU WOULD LIKE TO ADD UNDERWATER PARTS TO YOUR NESSY... HERE IS ONE WAY

ETC.

PENGUINS

THINGS in the WATER

THE WATER

SHARK GOING THIS WAY ←

GOING THAT WAY →

MEAN, HUNGRY SHARK LOOKING UP.

A WHALE

SNAKE SWIMMING

FROG PEEKING UP OUT OF THE WATER

ALLIGATOR SWIMMING

SWAN SWIMMING

DOG SWIMMING (DOING THE "DOG PADDLE")

DUCK DIVING DOWN FOR FOOD

TURTLE SWIMMING

WHALE'S TAIL

ETC.   ETC.

ANOTHER FROG PEEKING

SEAL IN THE WATER LOOKING AT YOU

ALLIGATOR (MEAN AND HUNGRY) LOOKING UP OUT OF THE WATER

PENGUIN LOOKING UP OUT OF THE WATER

PENGUIN DIVING DOWN UNDER THE WATER

DUCK SWIMMING

QUACKING

OTHER WATER ⟶

ETC

PERSON TREADING WATER

PERSON CALLING FOR HELP

HELP

ETC

SCUBA DIVER

PERSON DIVING INTO THE WATER

PERSON SWIMMING

ETC

PERSON DOING THE AUSTRALIAN CRAWL

ETC

FAT MAN FLOATING IN THE WATER

PANDAS

17

IF YOU LOOK
AT THE POODLE *
PAGES AND THE
** GINSFORTWOOZELLFIMM
PAGES YOU WILL
SEE SOME
IDEAS FOR OTHER
THINGS YOU CAN
DO WITH YOUR
PANDAS.

* POODLES, 22
** GINSFORTWOOZELLFIMMS 91

18

19

HI DIDDLE DIDDLE
THE CAT AND
THE FIDDLE

THE COW JUMPED
OVER THE MOON

THE LITTLE DOG
LAUGHED
TO SEE SUCH FUN

AND
THE DISH RAN AWAY
WITH THE SPOON

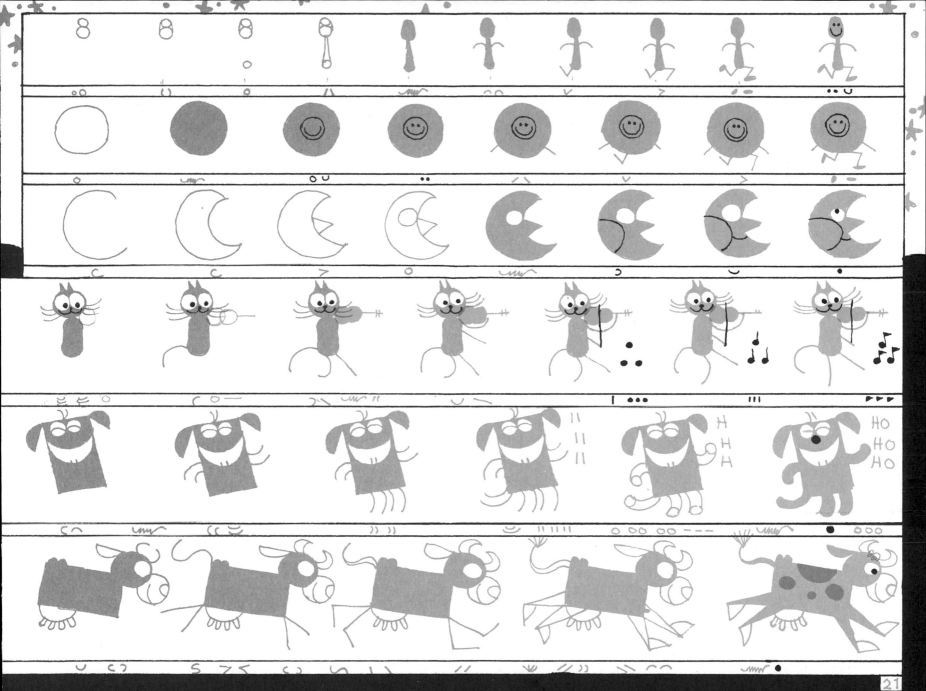

POODLES

22

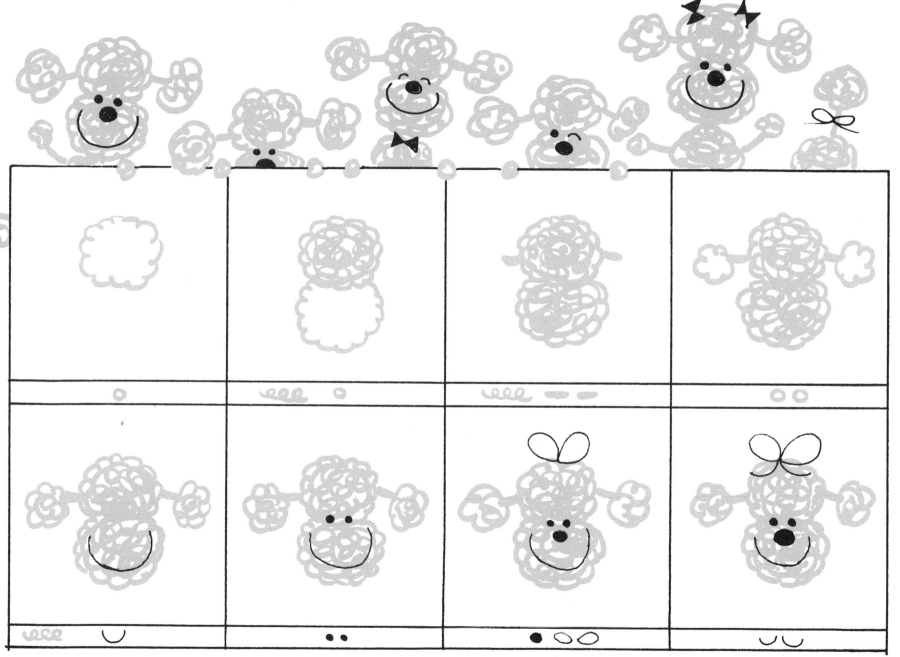

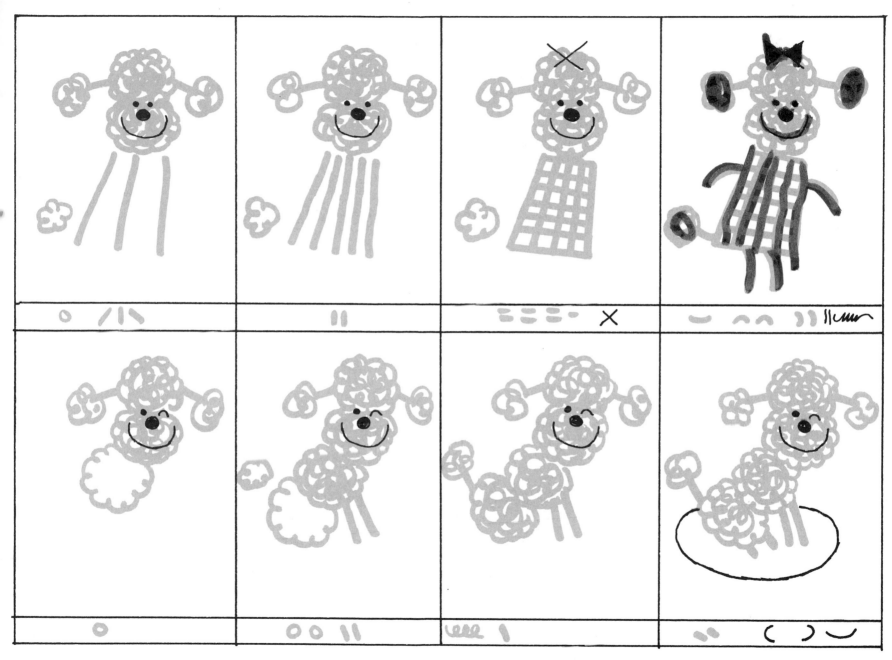

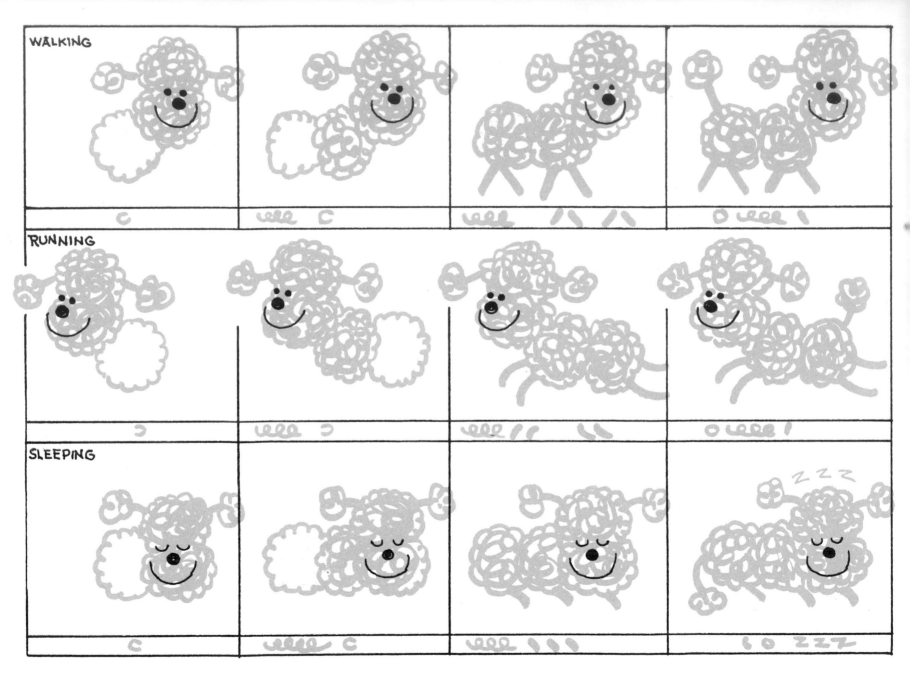

WALKING

RUNNING

SLEEPING

26

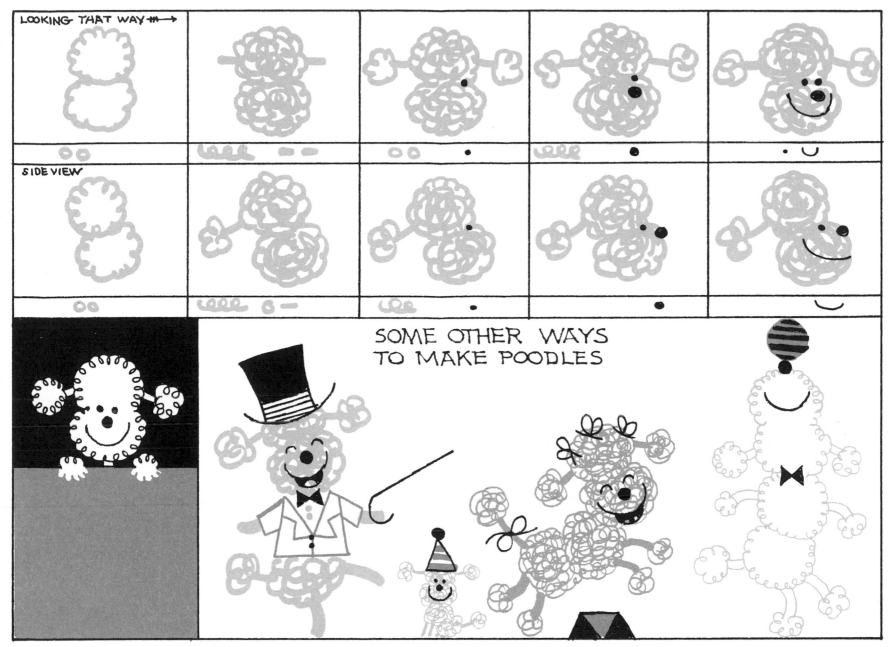

SOME OTHER WAYS
TO MAKE POODLES

27

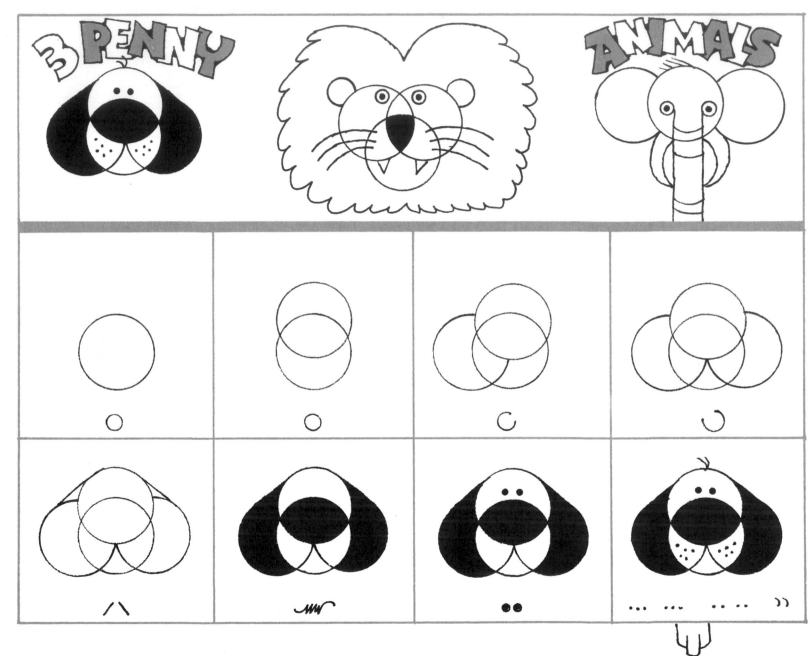

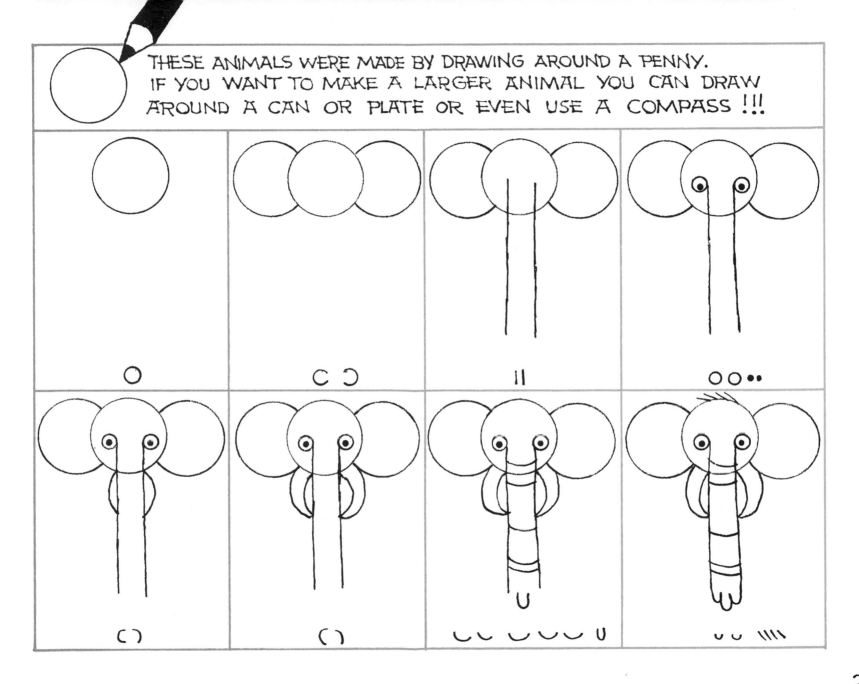

THESE ANIMALS WERE MADE BY DRAWING AROUND A PENNY.
IF YOU WANT TO MAKE A LARGER ANIMAL YOU CAN DRAW
AROUND A CAN OR PLATE OR EVEN USE A COMPASS !!!

THINGS PIRATICAL

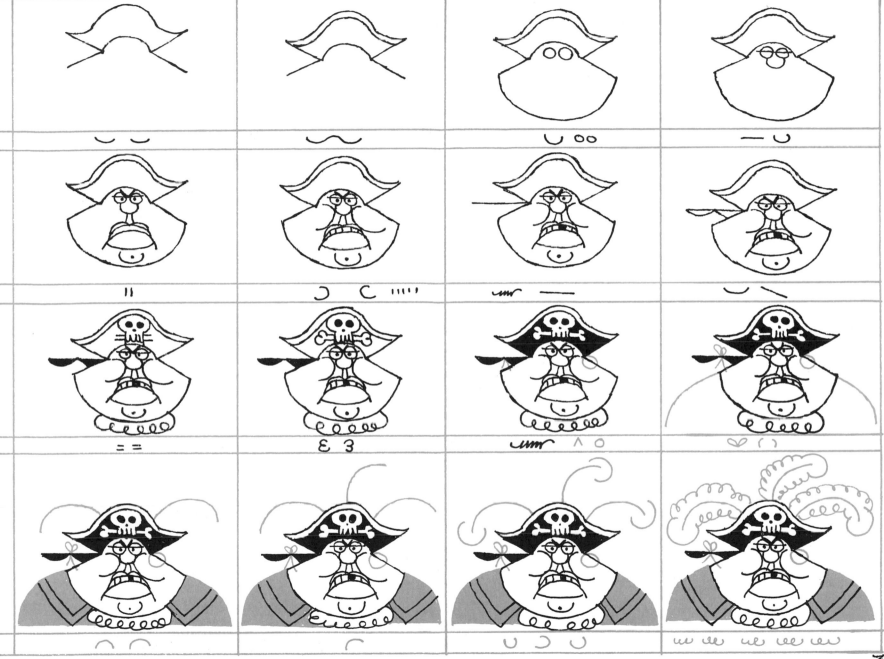

33

FLEABANE

34

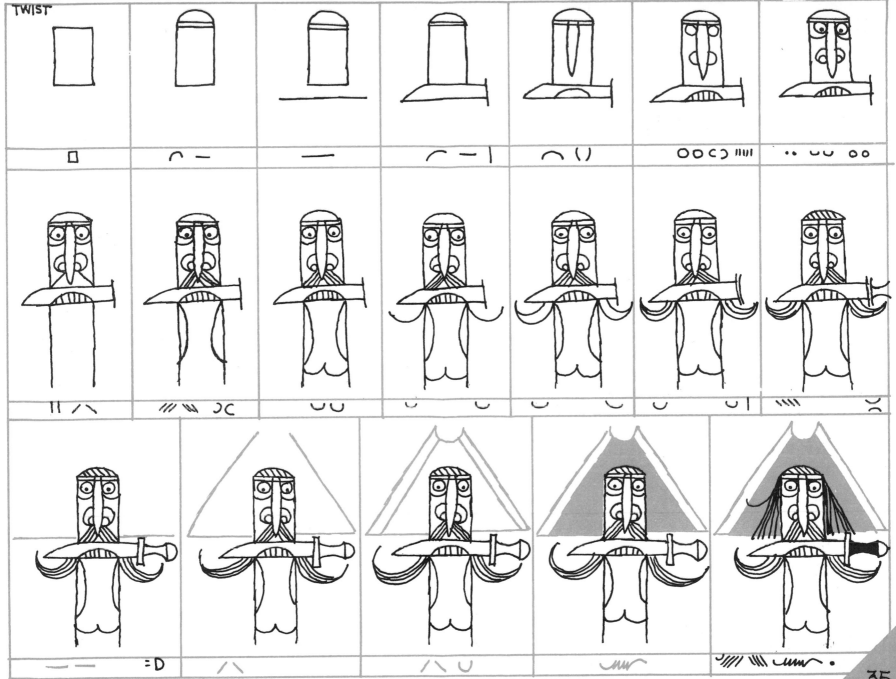

CHEST

RIGHT ARM

FOR HAND ➤➤→
SEE PAGE 38.

LEGS

BOOTS ETC.

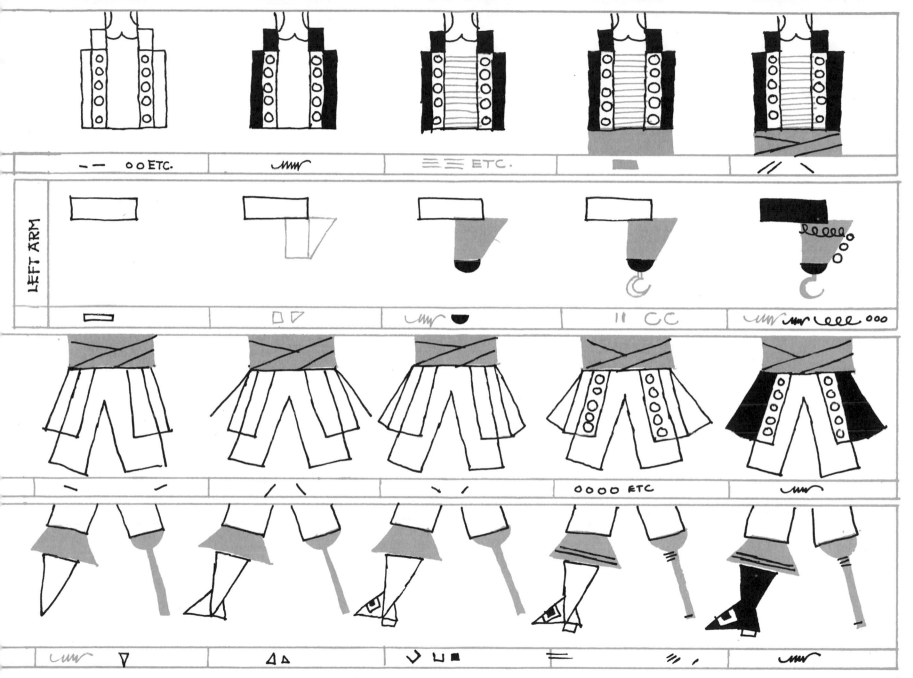

LEFT ARM

37

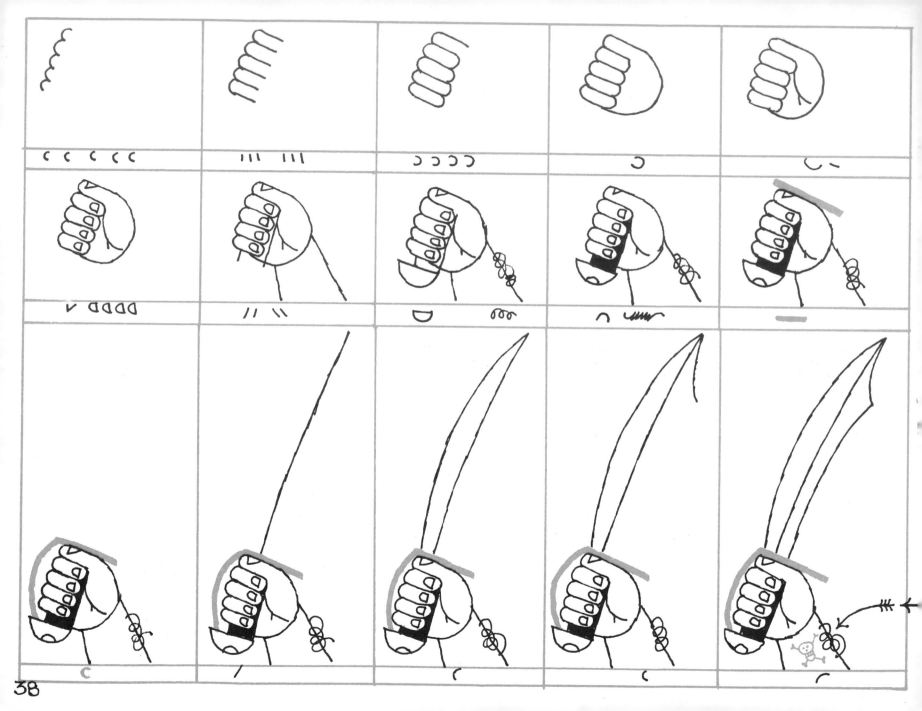

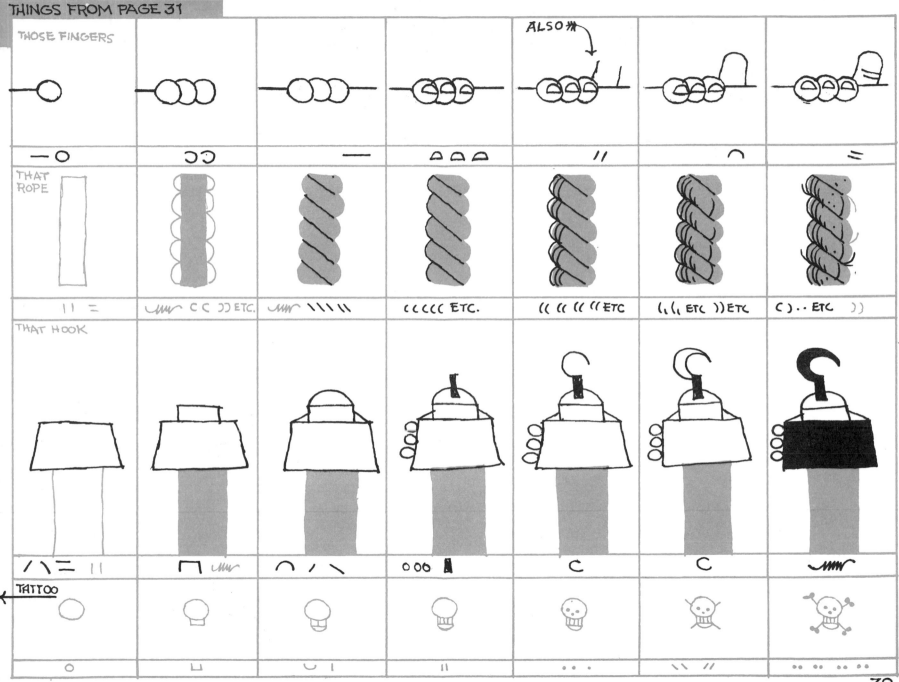

THOSE FINGERS

ALSO

—O   CC   —   ∩∩∩   //   ∩   =

THAT ROPE

|| =   ∼∼∼ C C)) ETC.   ∼∼∼ \\\\\\   (((((ETC.   ((((((((ETC   (, (, ETC)) ETC   C).. ETC))

THAT HOOK

/\ = || ⊓ ∼∼   ∩ /\   ∘∘∘ ▮   C   C   ∼∼∼

TATTOO

∘   ⊔   ∪ | || .. .   \\ //   .. ..

PRATE'S PISTOL

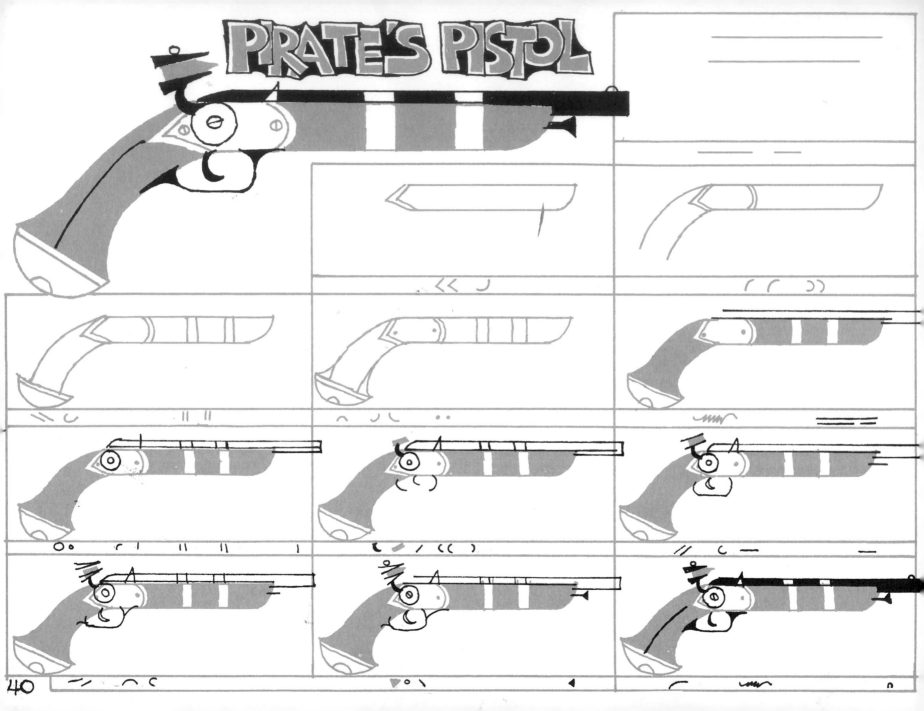

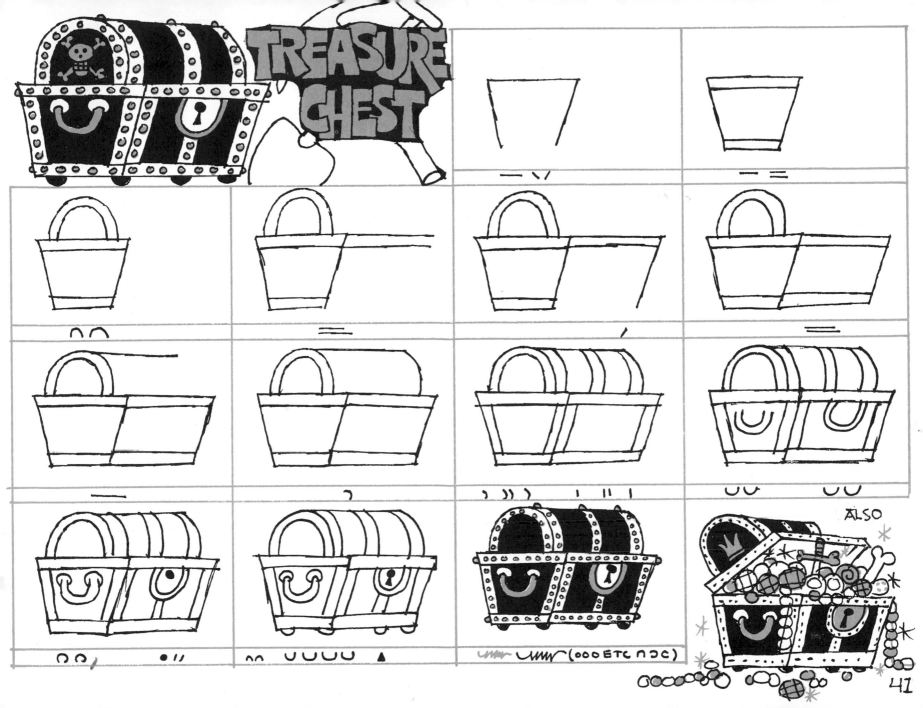

TREASURE CHEST

ALSO

41

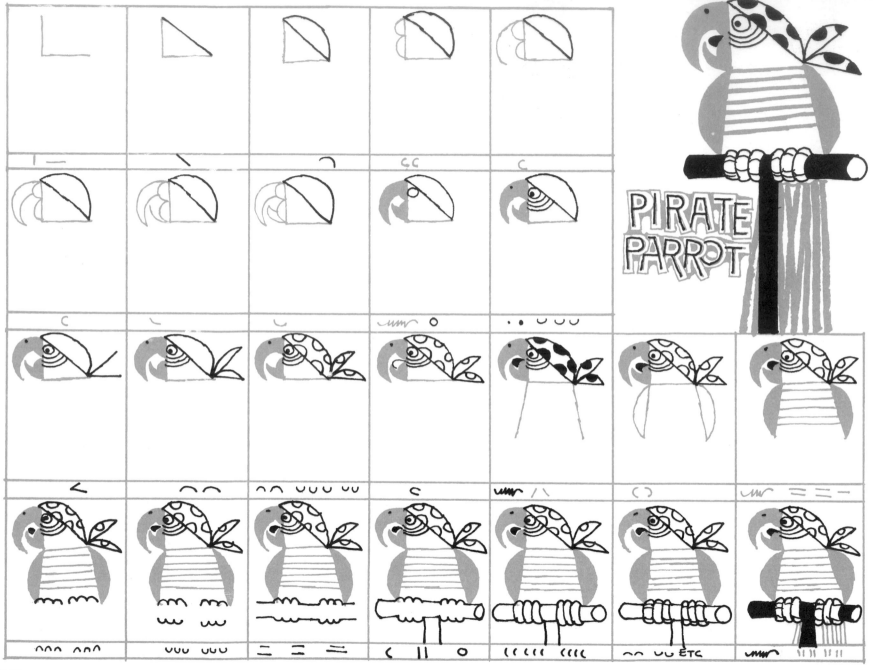

PIRATE
PARROT

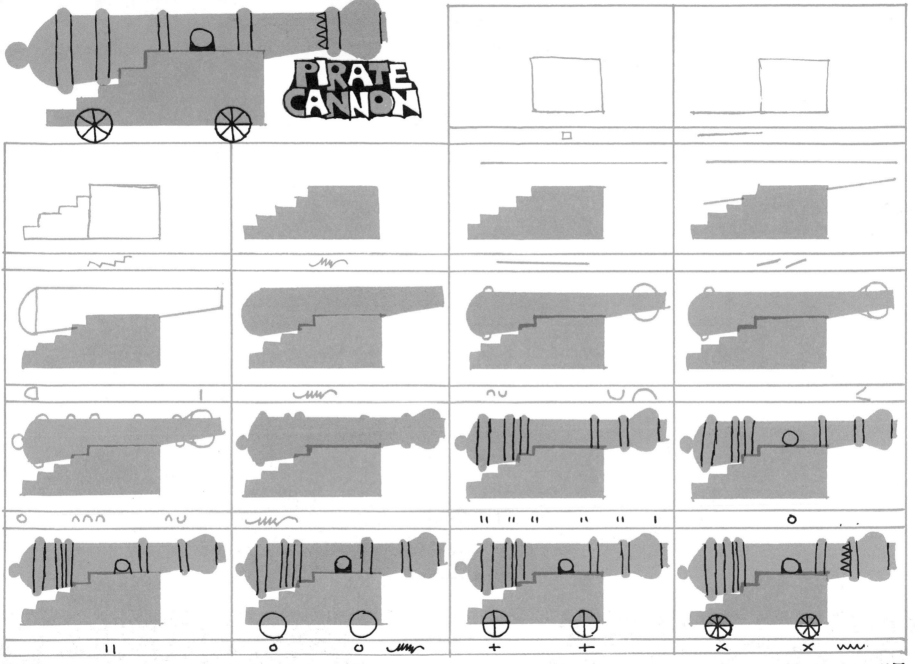

PIRATE CANNON

43

Sea Hawk

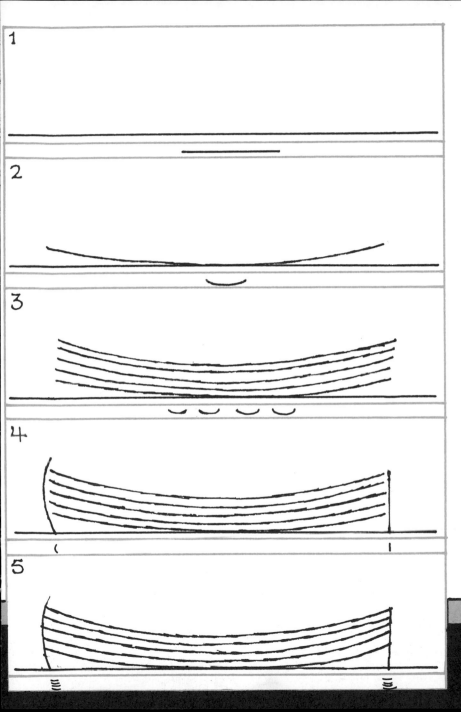

1

2

3

4

5

I FIND IT EASIER TO DRAW BACK AND FORTH LINES ⟷ THAN UP AND DOWN LINES ... ↕ SO, WHEN I HAVE TO DRAW LONG, STRAIGHT, UP AND DOWN LINES I OFTEN TURN MY PAPER AROUND LIKE THIS.

IF MY LINES ARE STILL NOT AS STRAIGHT AS I WOULD LIKE I USE A STRAIGHT EDGE SUCH AS A RULER OR A PIECE OF CARDBOARD.

AN OLD PAD BACK MAKES A GOOD STRAIGHT EDGE.

TILTED MASTS

TRIANGLE

"T" SQUARE

IF I AM WORRIED ABOUT MY MASTS BEING TILTED (SOMETIMES I DO, SOMETIMES I DO NOT) I WILL USE A "T" SQUARE AND A TRIANGLE ... IF I DO NOT HAVE THESE TOOLS I USE THE CORNER OF AN OLD PAD BACK, LIKE THIS.

DECIDE WHERE YOU WANT TO PUT YOUR MASTS.

LINE ONE EDGE OF PAD BACK UP WITH WATERLINE.

DRAW ALONG THE OTHER EDGE.

VOILA !!!

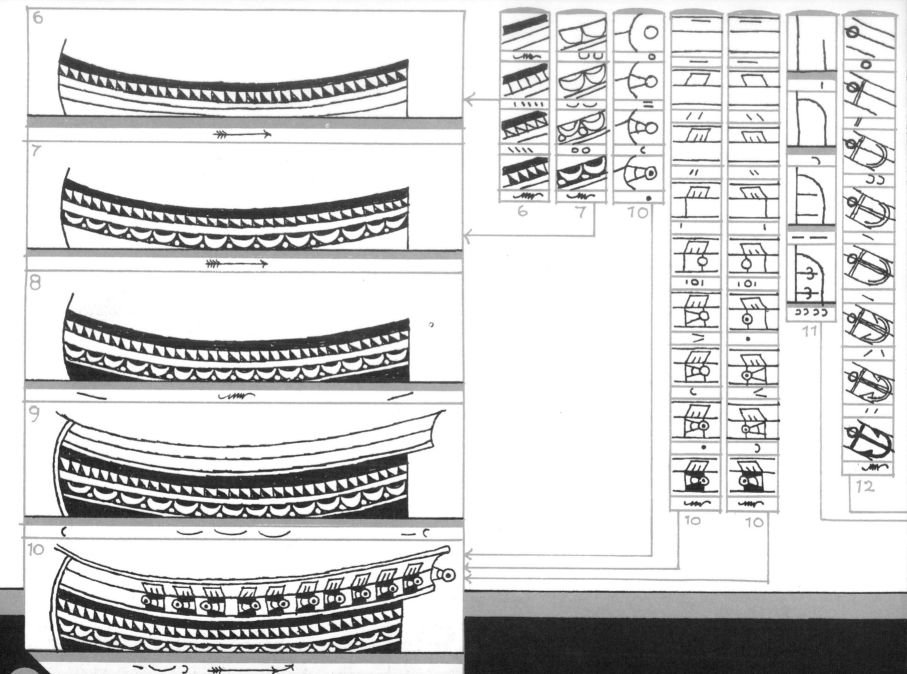

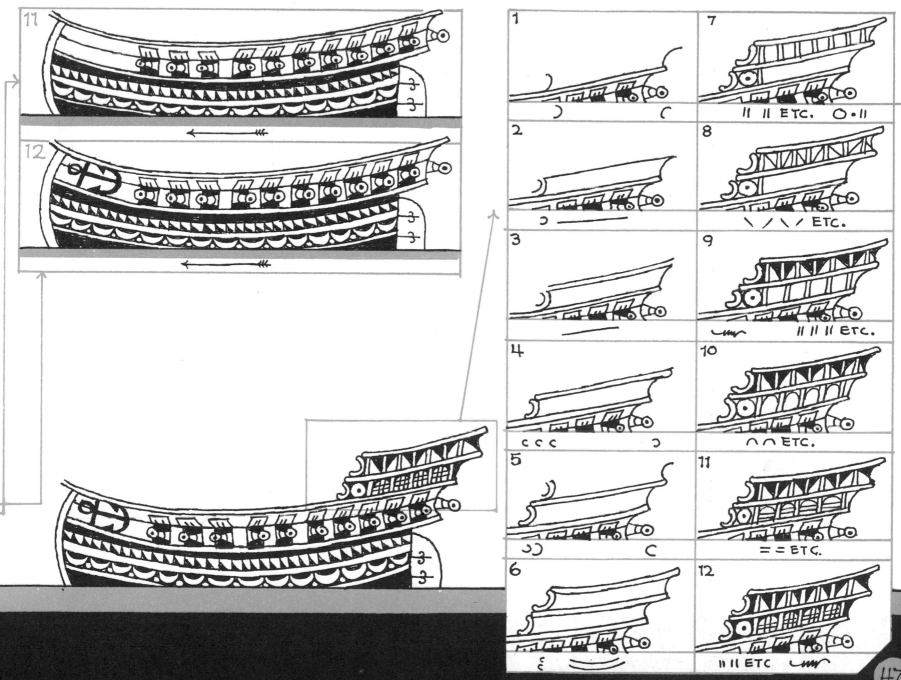

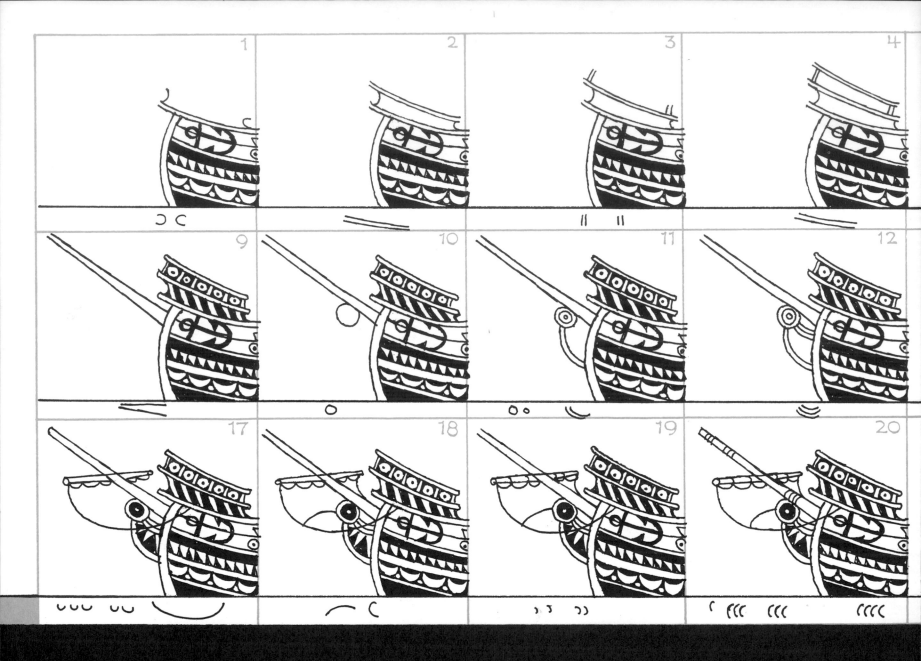

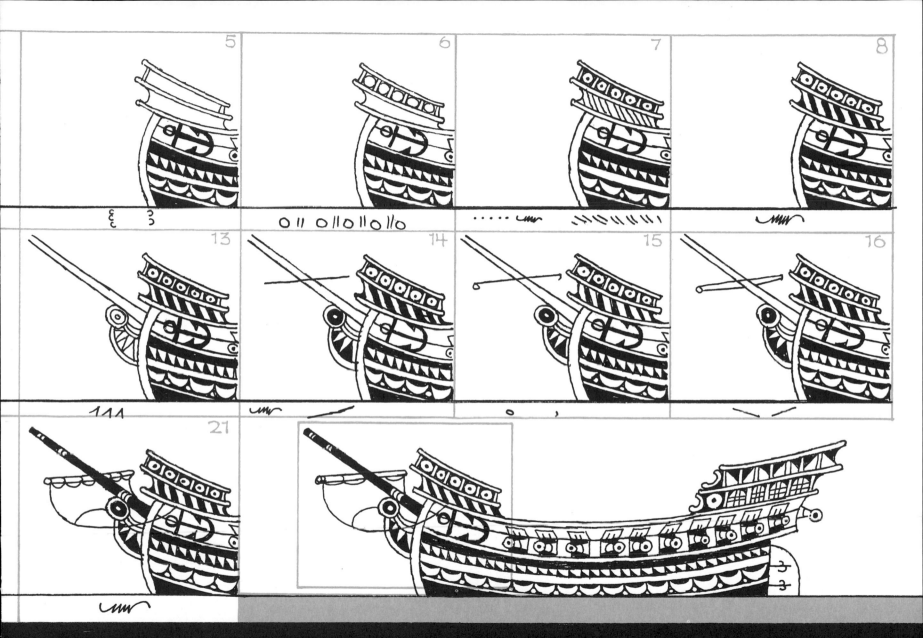

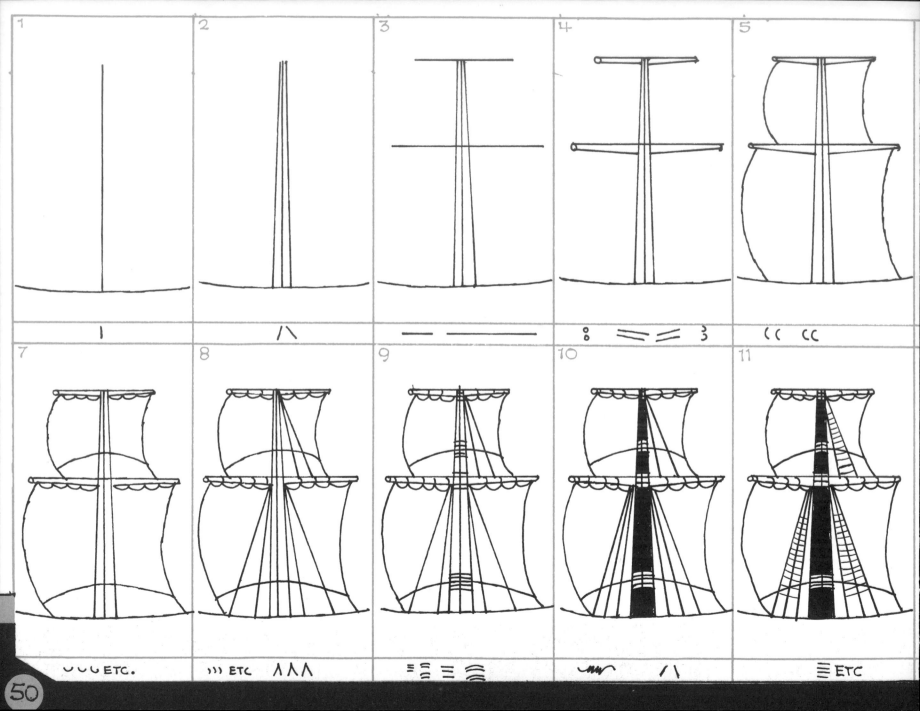

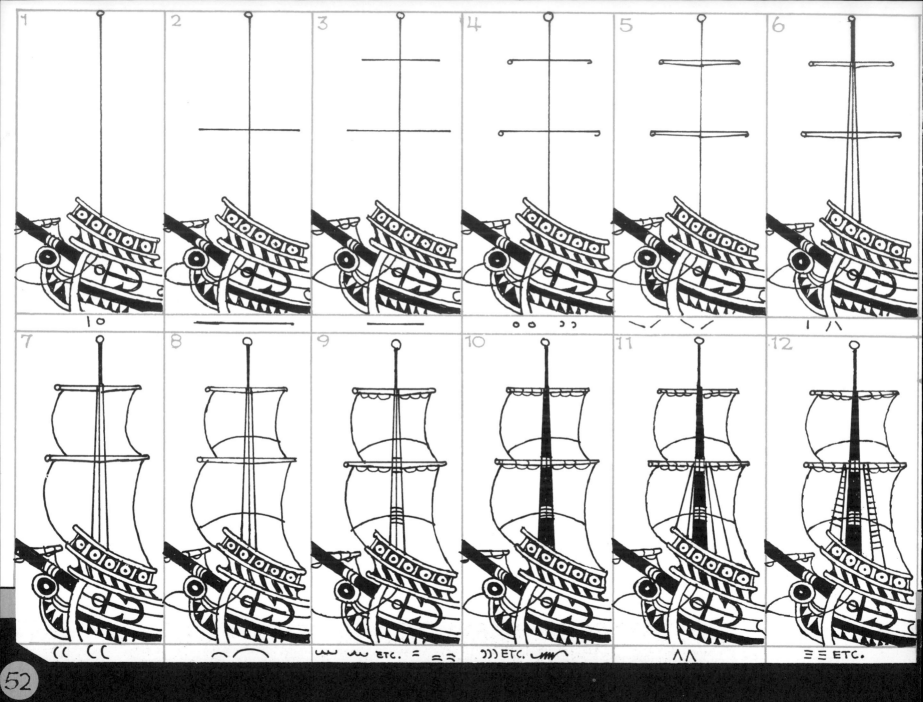

ETC.

ETC.

ALSO

53

IF YOU LOOK CAREFULLY
YOU WILL SEE THAT THIS DRAWING
DOES NOT MATCH THE INSTRUCTIONS EXACTLY
IN EVERY DETAIL. (I FIND IT HARD TO DRAW
A THING THE SAME WAY TWICE)

THERE ARE MANY WAYS YOU CAN CHANGE THE "SEA HAWK" TO "BUILD" A DIFFERENT
SHIP. FOR INSTANCE, YOU CAN ADD MORE MASTS, SAILS OR ROWS OF CANNON.
YOU CAN CHANGE THE DECORATIONS AND/OR COLOR. YOU CAN USE
STRAIGHT LINES FOR THE HULL. USING THIS BASIC IDEA YOU CAN
MAKE YOUR OWN NAVY, FLEET OR ARMADA!

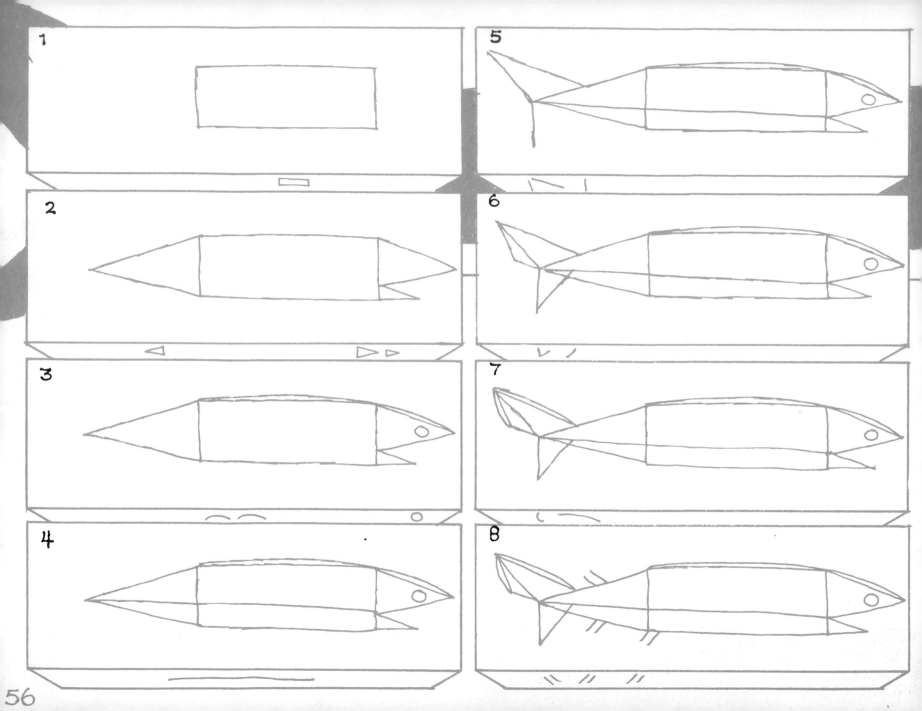

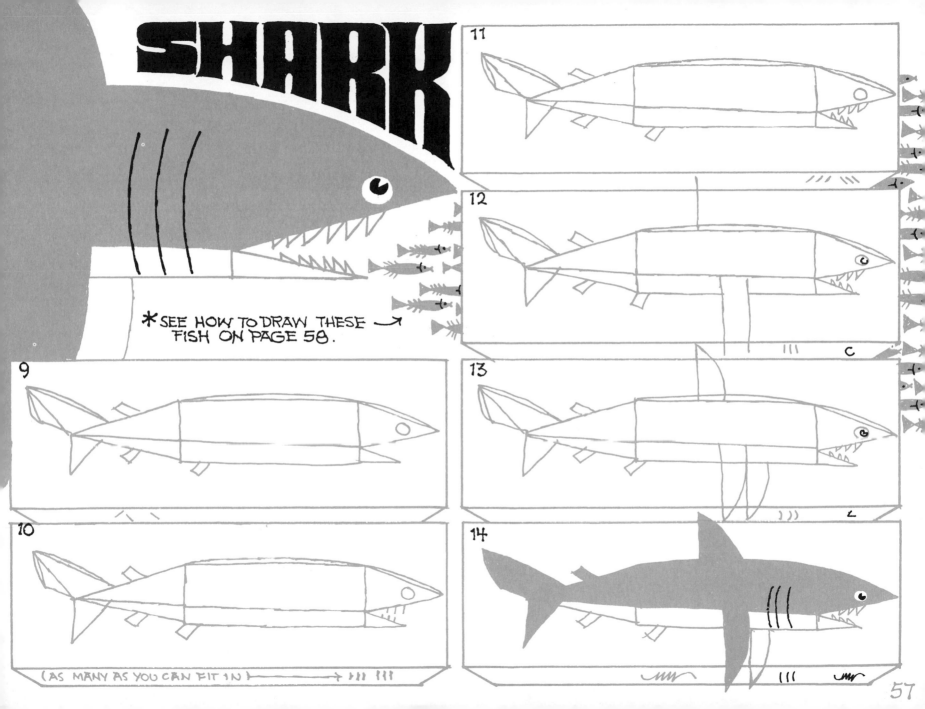

SHARK

* SEE HOW TO DRAW THESE → FISH ON PAGE 58.

9

10

(AS MANY AS YOU CAN FIT IN) →))))))

11

12

C

13

14

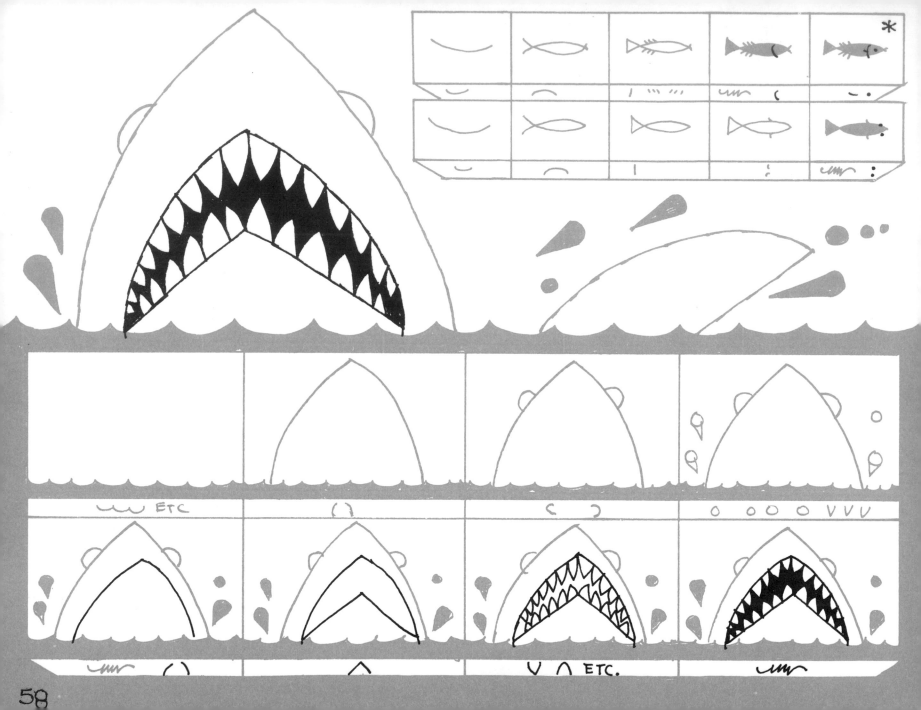

ETC

( )

C)

O O O O V V V

ᴜᴡ ETC.

V Λ ETC.

58

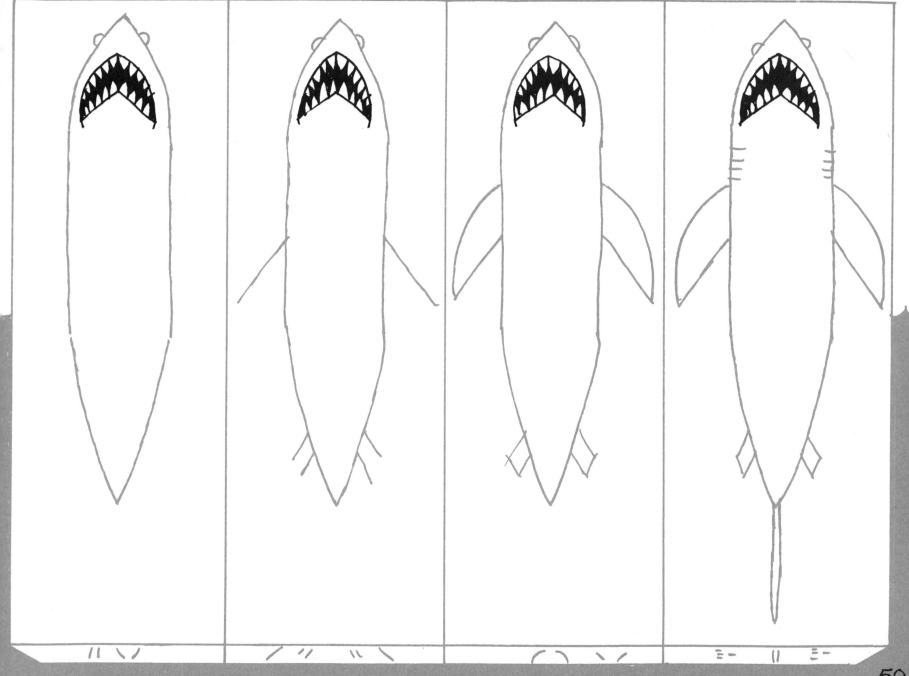

59

DEM BUGZIZ

BEE   FLY

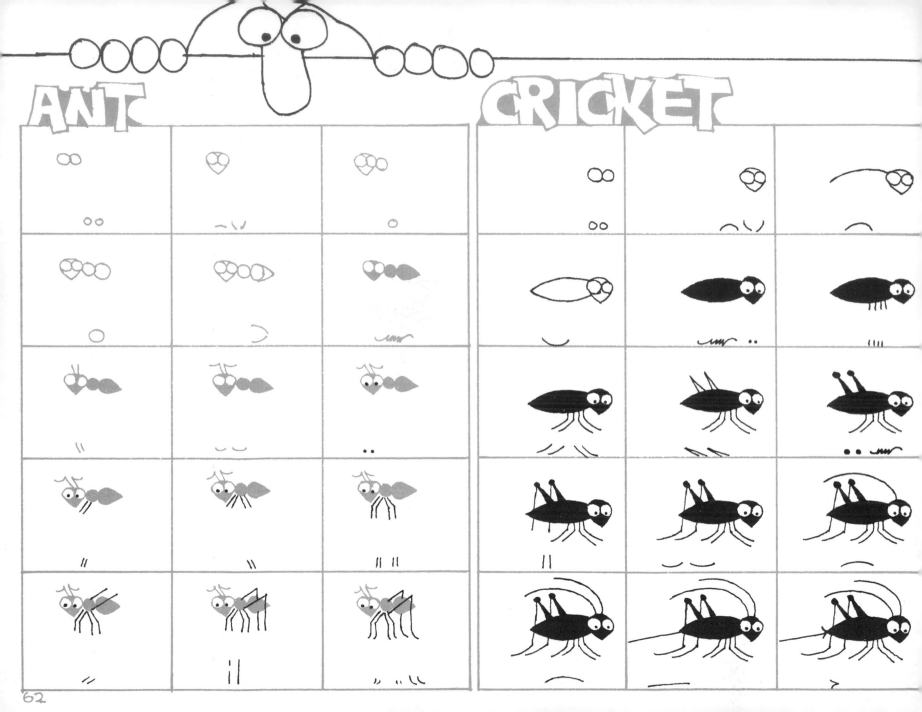

SPIDER   GRASSHOPPER

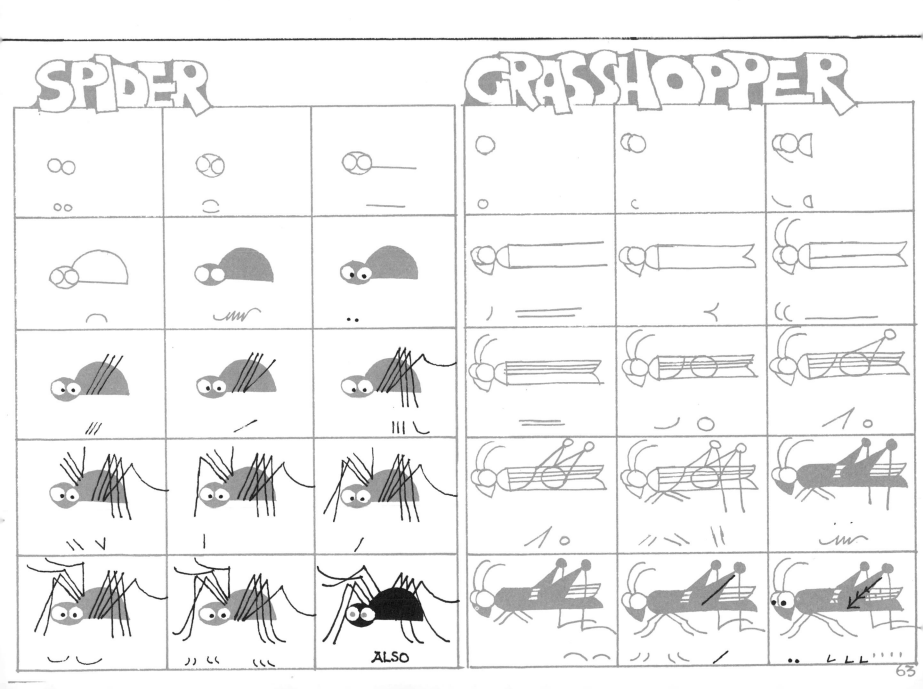

ALSO

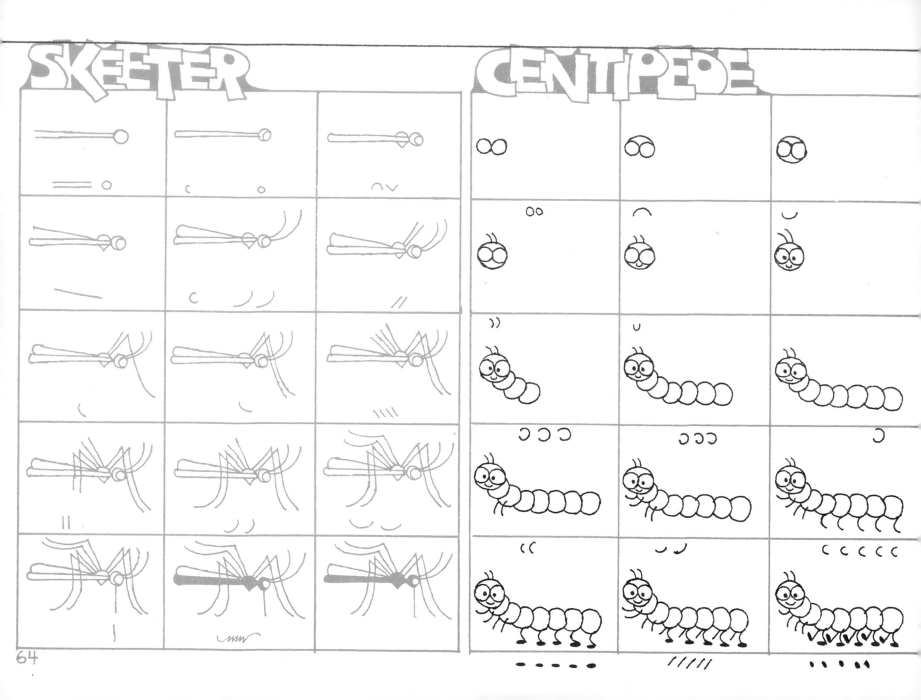

SWAMP CREATURE

*"DRACULA" IS IN THE BIG GREEN DRAWING BOOK.

MORE CREATURES IN THE BIG ORANGE DRAWING BOOK.

== ← AS MANY AS YOU NEED   ⦀⦀⦀   ⦀⦀⦀   ∪∪∪∪∪ ETC.   ⦀⦀ ⊘   ∪∪∪ ETC. ⋎⋎⋎

67

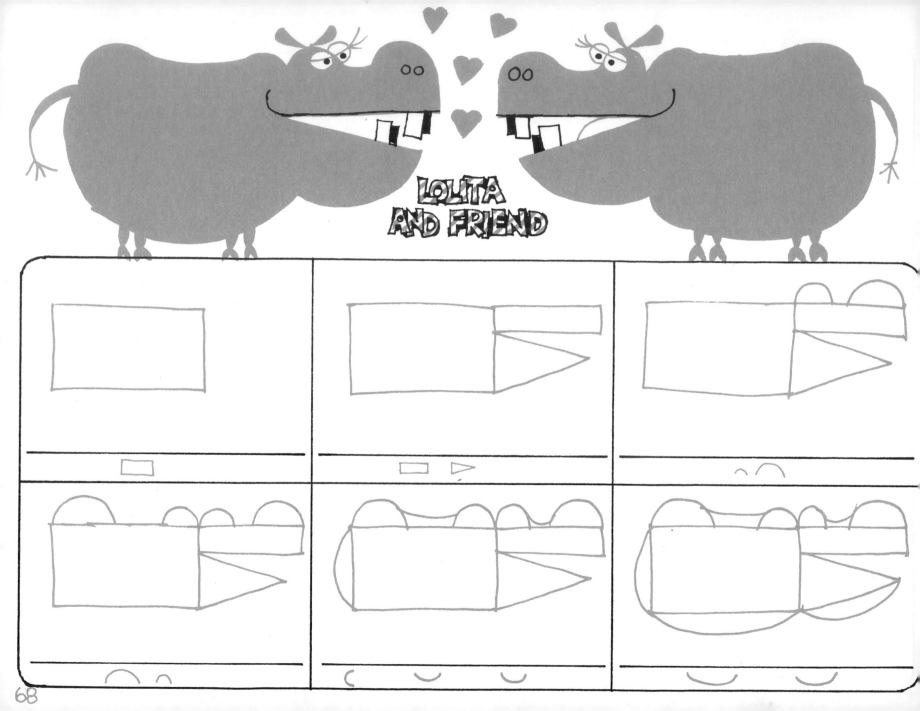

LOLITA
AND FRIEND

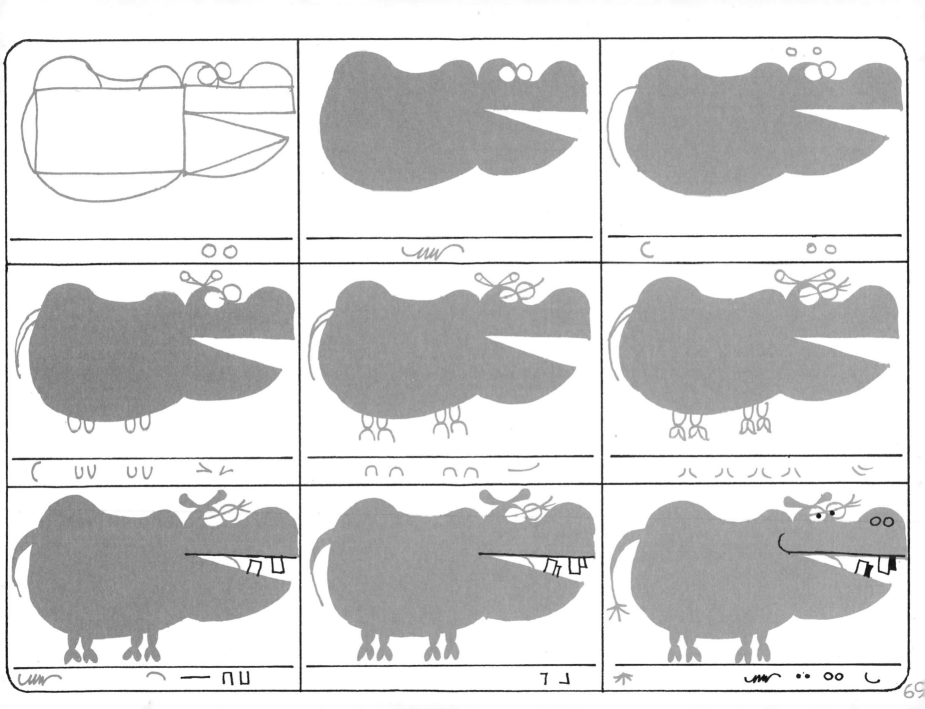

69

OTHER LESS GRAND BUT VERY NICE HIPPOS

SWIMMING   SWIMMING   DEAD HIPPO   YAWNING

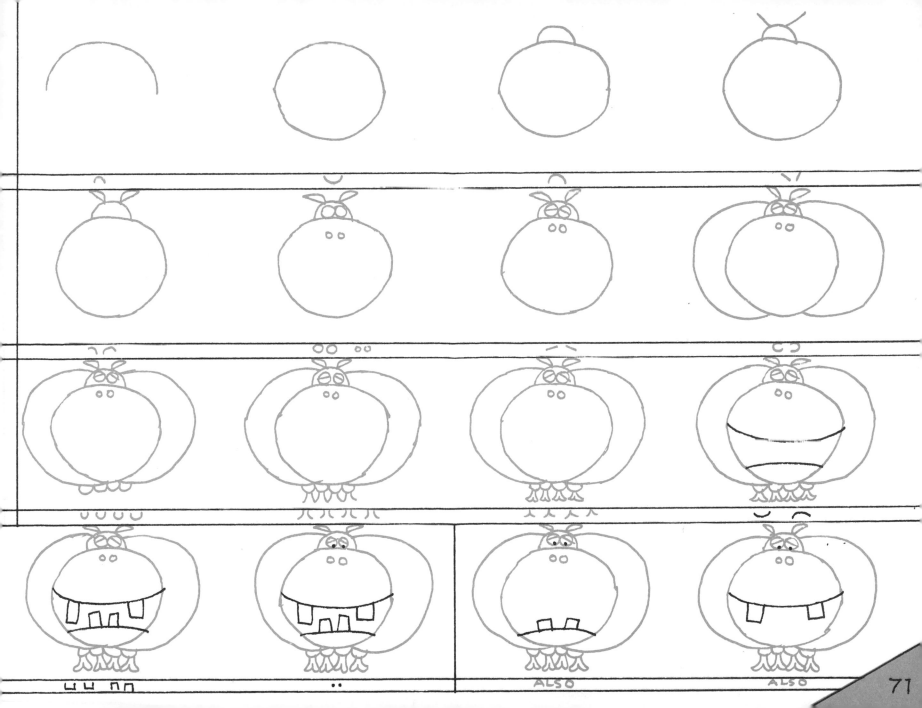

ALSO ALSO

71

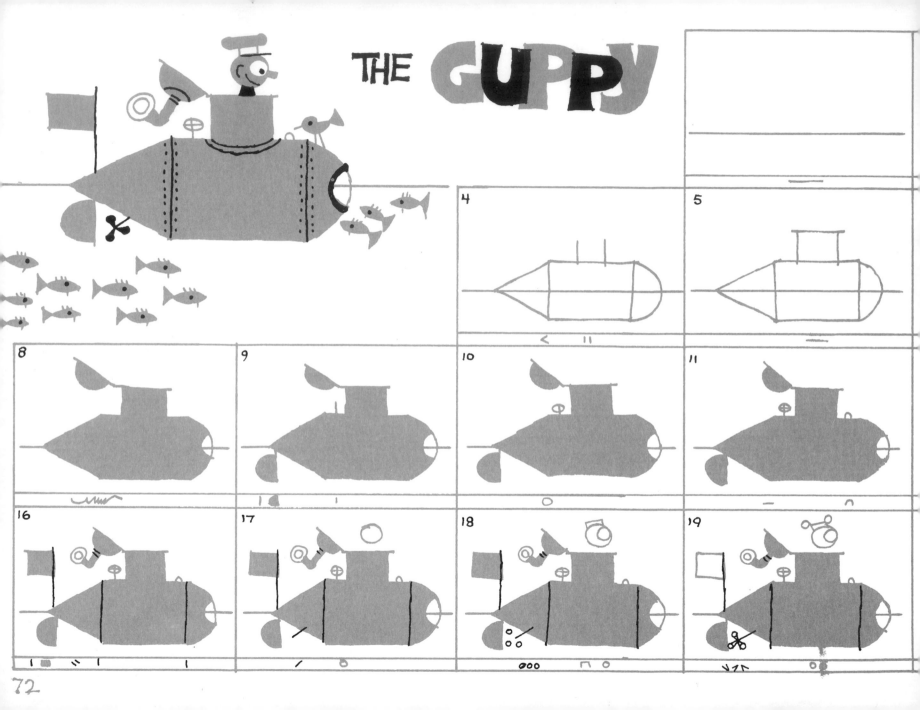

THE GUPPY

4

5

8

9

10

11

16

17

18

19

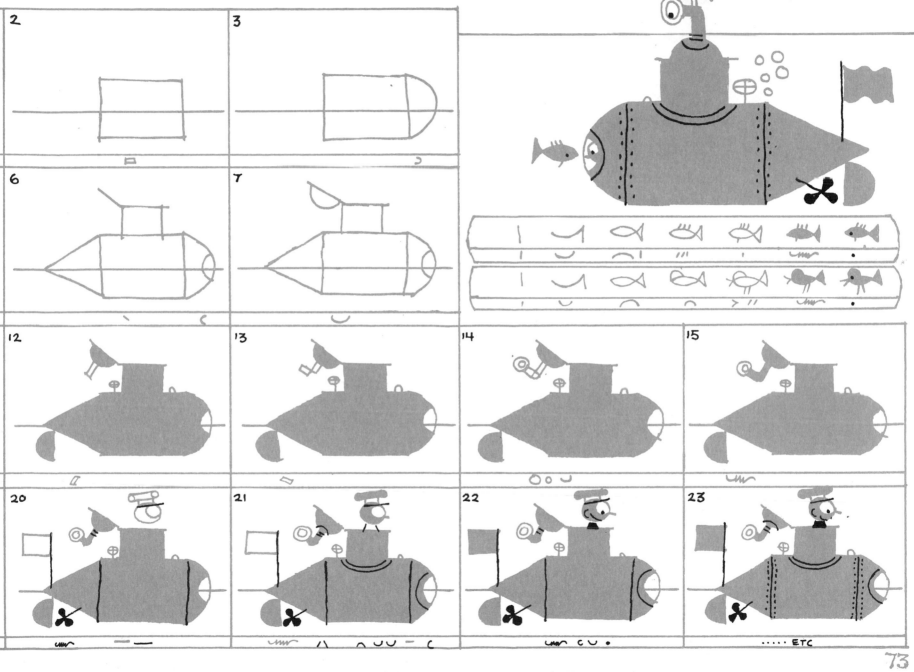

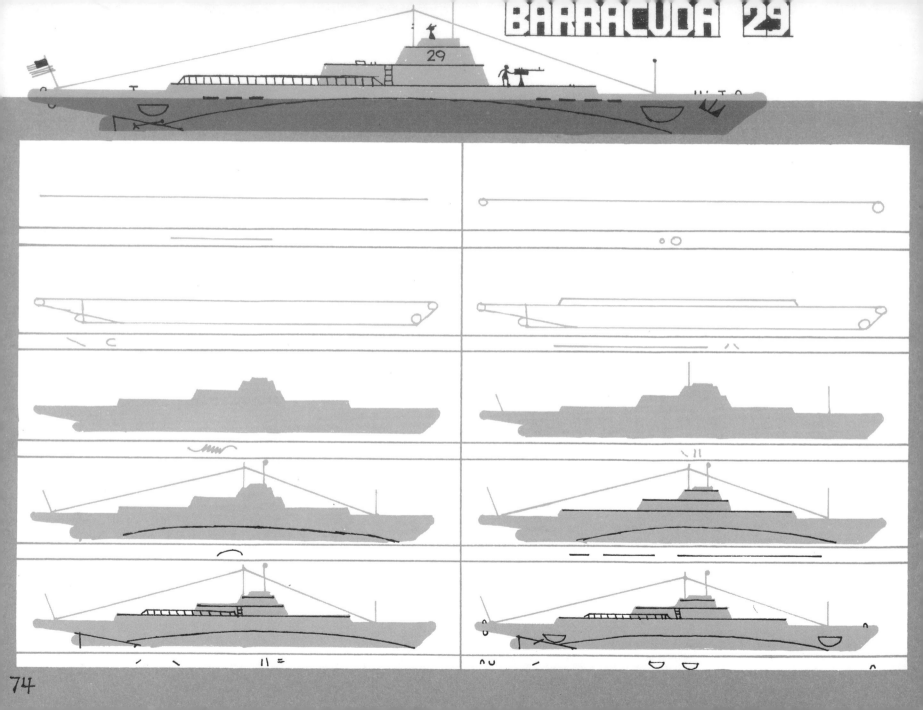

BARRACUDA 29

29

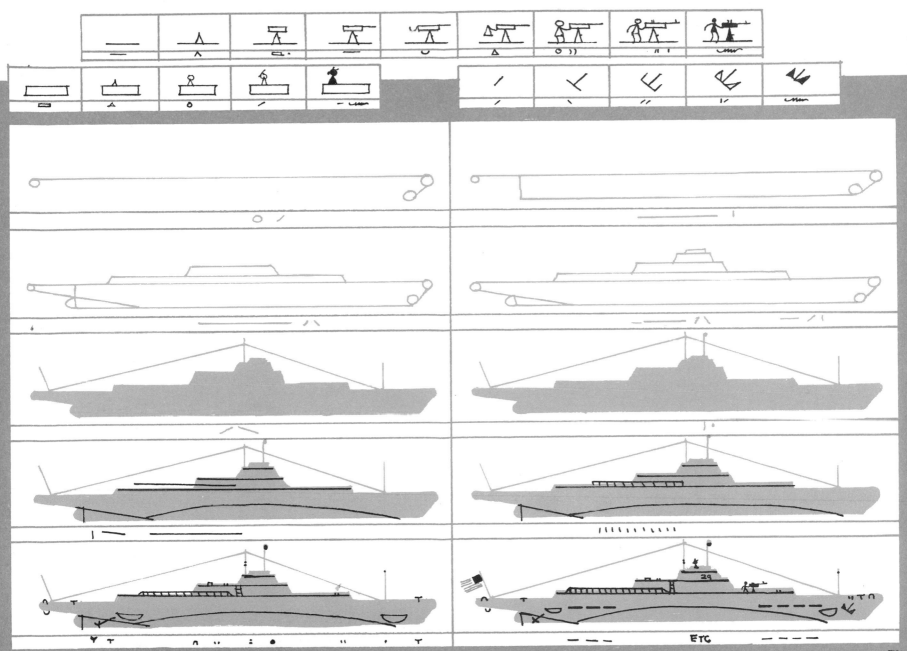

75

40 YEARS AGO SOMEONE SHOWED ME HOW
TO DRAW THESE 3 THINGS.
I STILL REMEMBER HOW TO DRAW THEM.
DRAWING THEM TURNED A LITTLE LIGHT ON
IN MY MIND, GAVE ME MANY HOURS OF PLEASURE
AND BECAME THE INSPIRATION FOR A SERIES
OF DRAWING BOOKS OF WHICH THIS IS ONE.
I FIGURED IT WAS ABOUT TIME THAT I
PASSED THEM ON. PERHAPS ONE DAY
SOME OF YOU WILL IN TURN PASS THEM ON
TO SOMEONE ELSE.

Ed Emberley IPSWICH, MASS. JAN. 1981

THAT SHIP

THAT SUB

THAT TANK

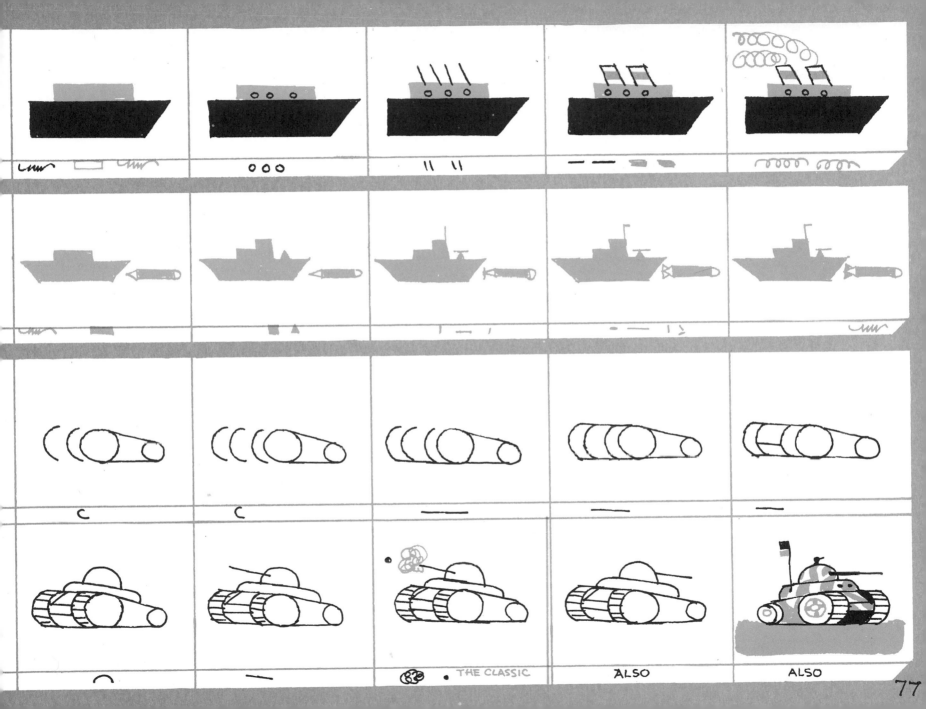

THE CLASSIC

ALSO

ALSO

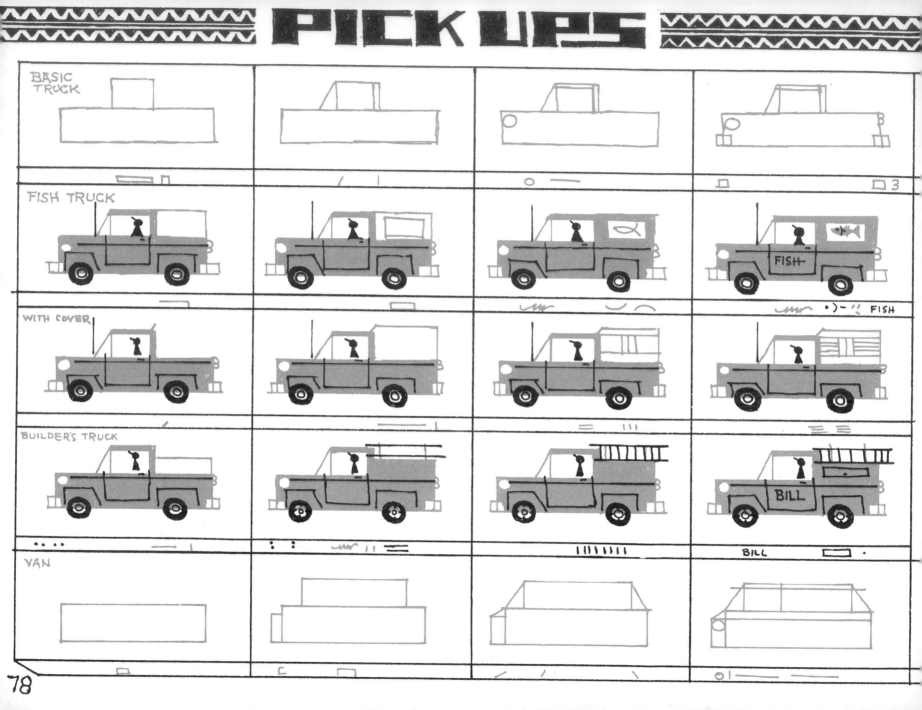

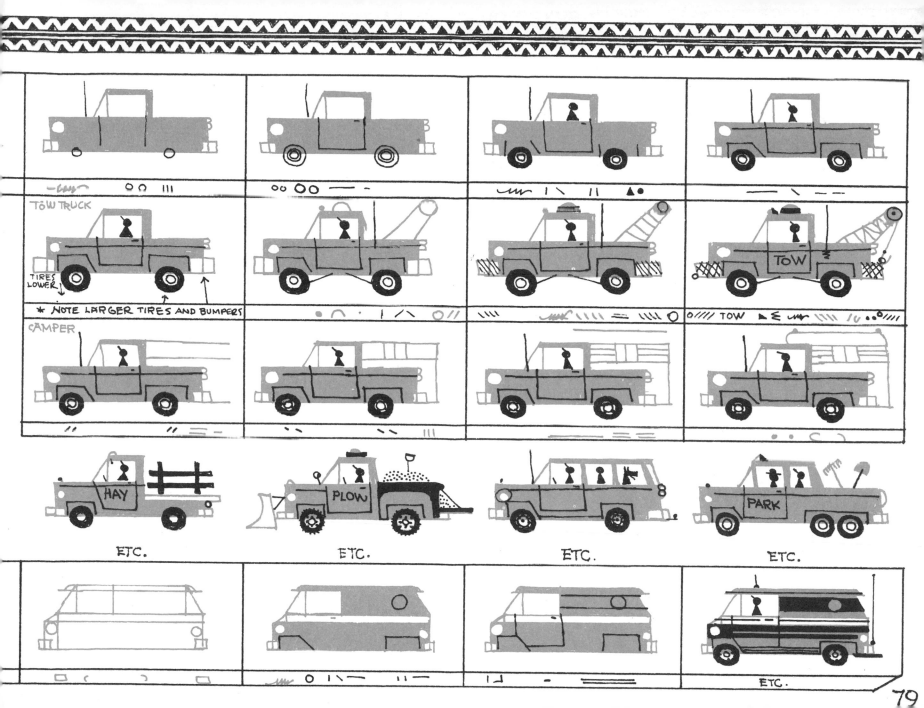

TOW TRUCK

TIRES LOWER

* NOTE LARGER TIRES AND BUMPERS

TOW

CAMPER

HAY

PLOW

PARK

ETC.

ETC.

ETC.

ETC.

ETC.

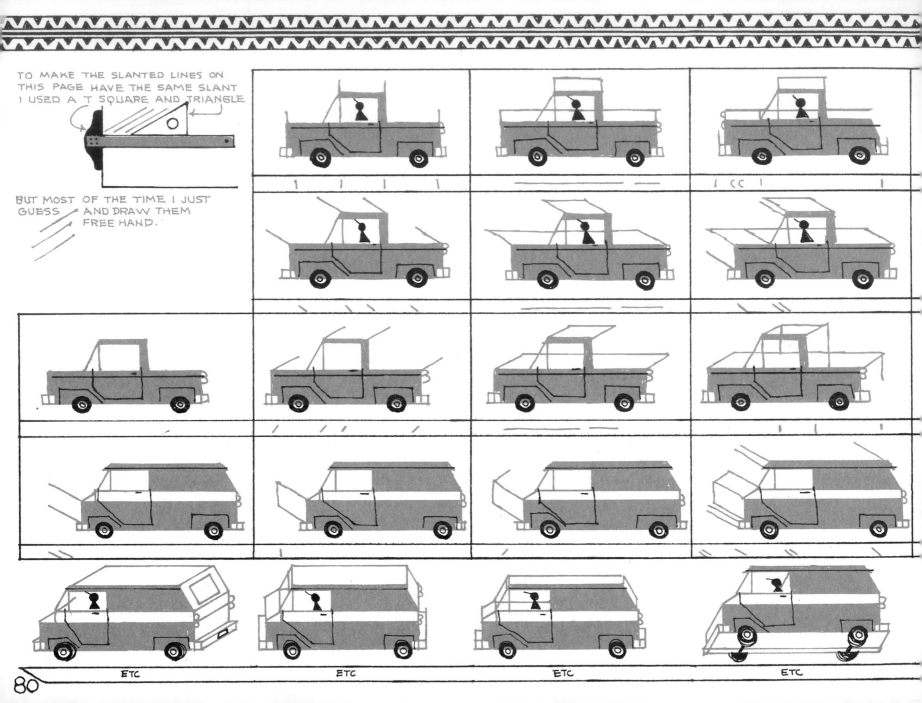

TO MAKE THE SLANTED LINES ON THIS PAGE HAVE THE SAME SLANT I USED A T SQUARE AND TRIANGLE

BUT MOST OF THE TIME I JUST GUESS AND DRAW THEM FREE HAND.

ETC   ETC   ETC   ETC

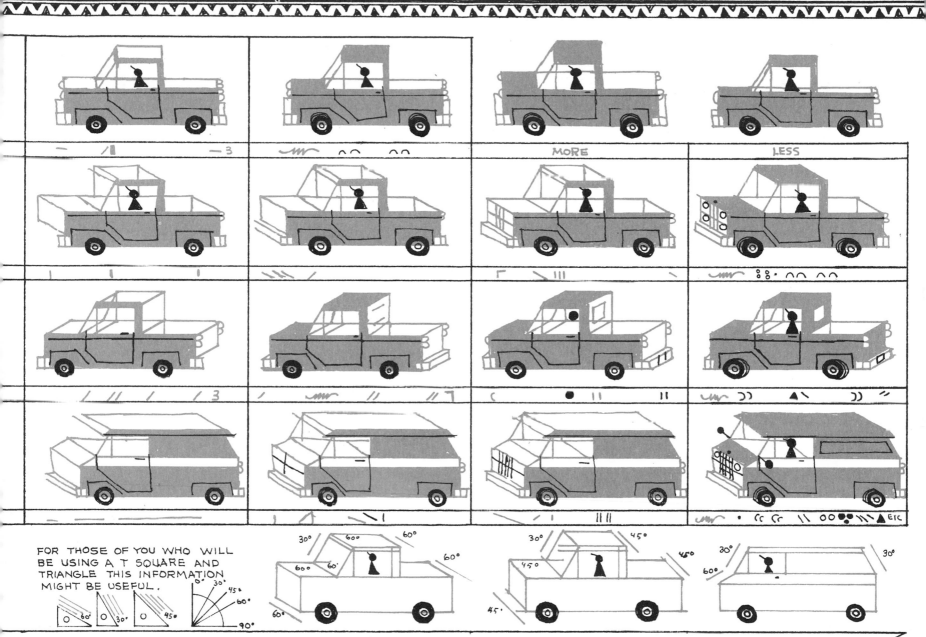

MORE

LESS

FOR THOSE OF YOU WHO WILL
BE USING A T SQUARE AND
TRIANGLE THIS INFORMATION
MIGHT BE USEFUL.

*NOTE NO HEADLIGHT & NO ANTENNA

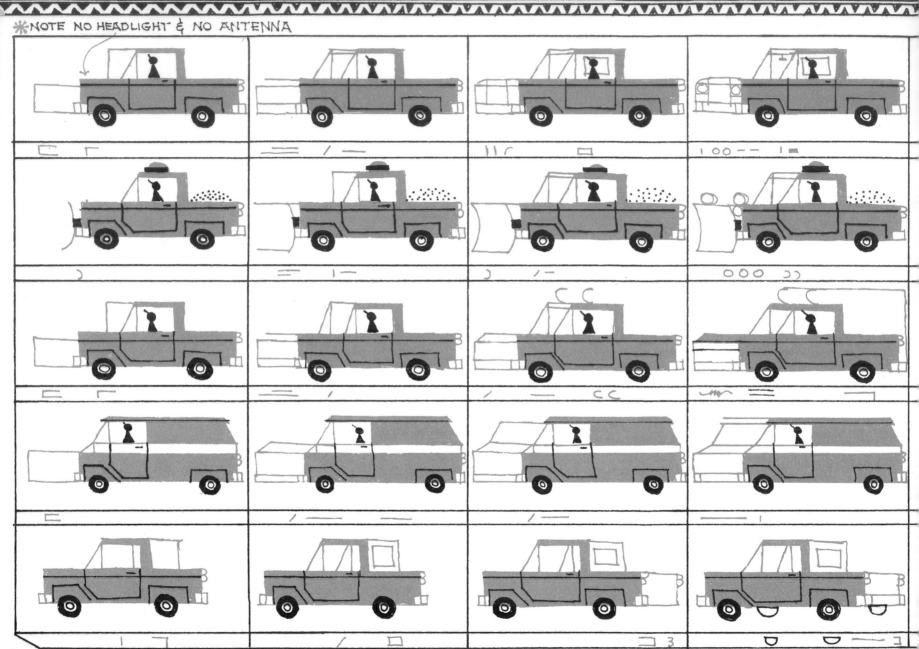

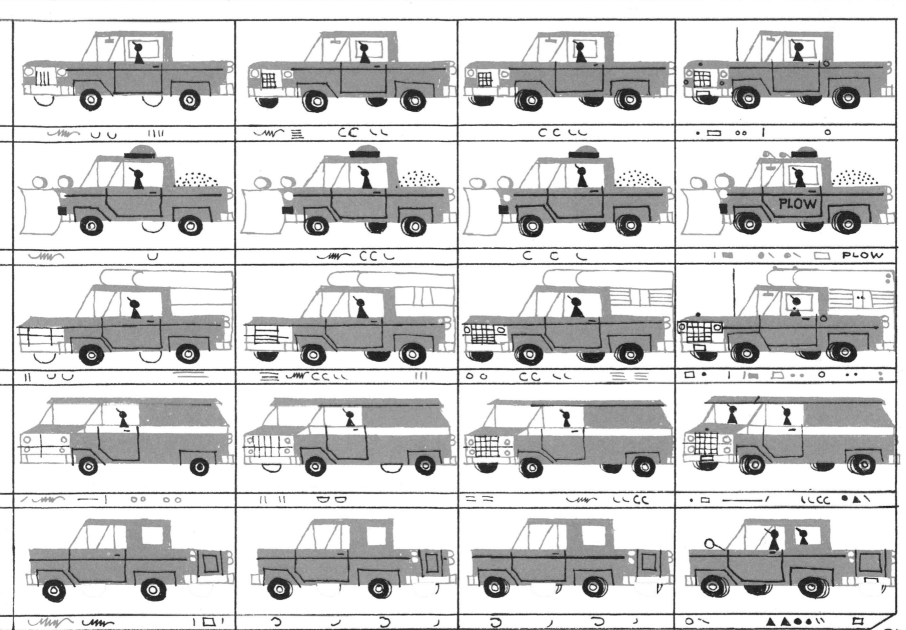

A NEEBORT
FROO

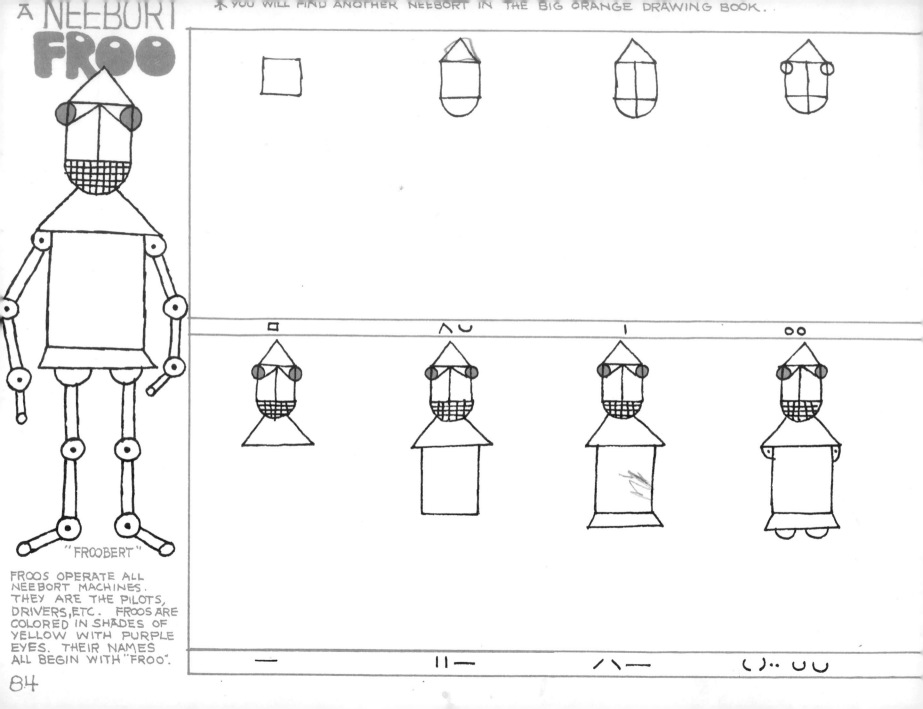

"FROOBERT"

FROOS OPERATE ALL
NEEBORT MACHINES.
THEY ARE THE PILOTS,
DRIVERS, ETC. FROOS ARE
COLORED IN SHADES OF
YELLOW WITH PURPLE
EYES. THEIR NAMES
ALL BEGIN WITH "FROO".

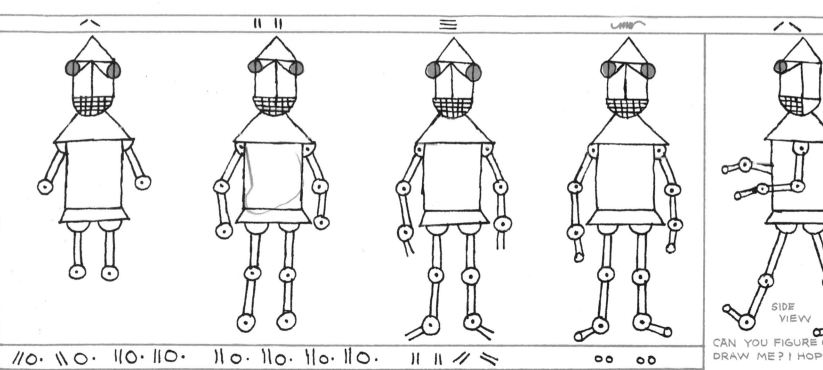

SIDE VIEW

CAN YOU FIGURE OUT HOW TO DRAW ME? I HOPE SO.

85

A FROOTER

THE MOST COMMON NEEBORT VEHICLE
IS A FROO SCOOTER (CALLED A FROOTER)
IT IS A 3 WHEELED 'ALL PURPOSE
VEHICLE USE FOR PICK UP AND
DELIVERY. IT HAS A NUMBER OF
TRAILERS AND OTHER USEFUL
ATTACHMENTS.
* FROOS HAVE THEIR OWN LIGHT FOR
SEEING IN THE DARK. THIS LIGHT IS
CALLED
FROOSEE.

1

2

FRONT VIEW

3

4

5

6

7

FROO
"FINGER"
FITS IN
SPECIAL
"CONTROL
HOLE."

FROO LEGS FOLD UP AND
FIT INSIDE A FROOTER.

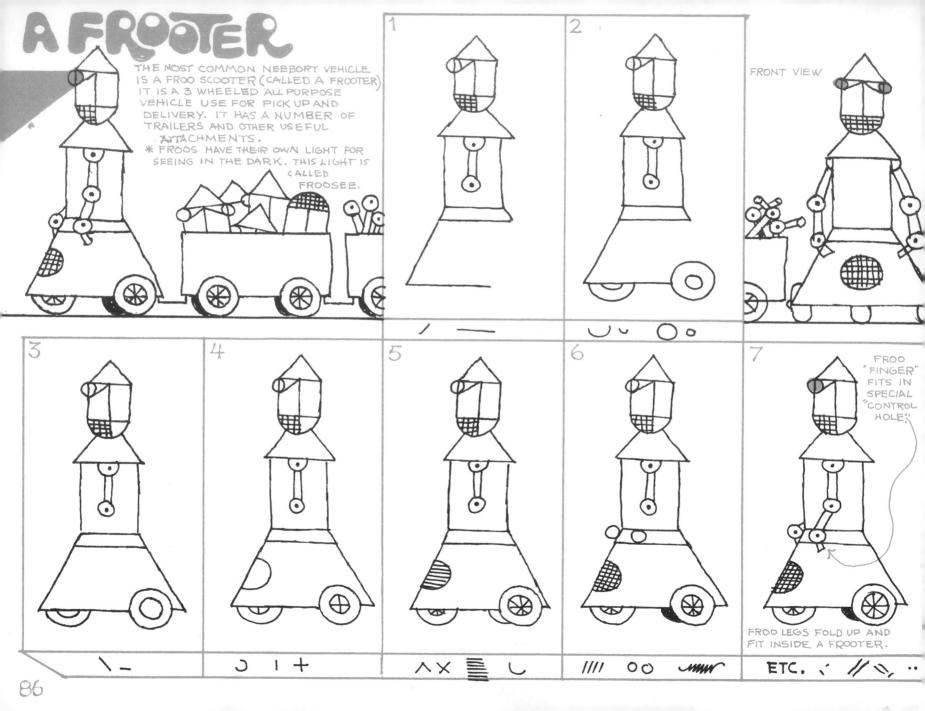

A NEEBORT TRAKIR

THESE HEAVY DUTY
BASIC UNITS ARE USED ALONE AND
ARE USED AS PARTS OF LARGER MACHINES
USED FOR EXPLORATION, MINING,
DEFENSE AND OTHER SIMILAR TASKS
SUCH AS EARTH MOVING. (CALLED ZORT
MOVING ON THE PLANET ZORT* AND
FRED MOVING ON FRED **)

* SEE PAGE 82 BIG GREEN DRAWING BOOK.
** SEE PAGE 91 THIS BOOK.

"KREEGOR..." A PATROL LEADER
NEEBORT—PG 86 BIG ORANGE
DRAWING BOOK.

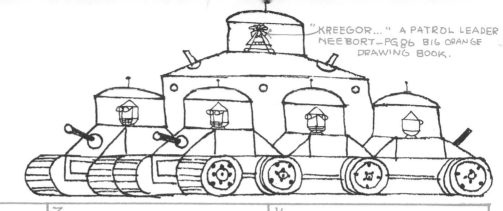

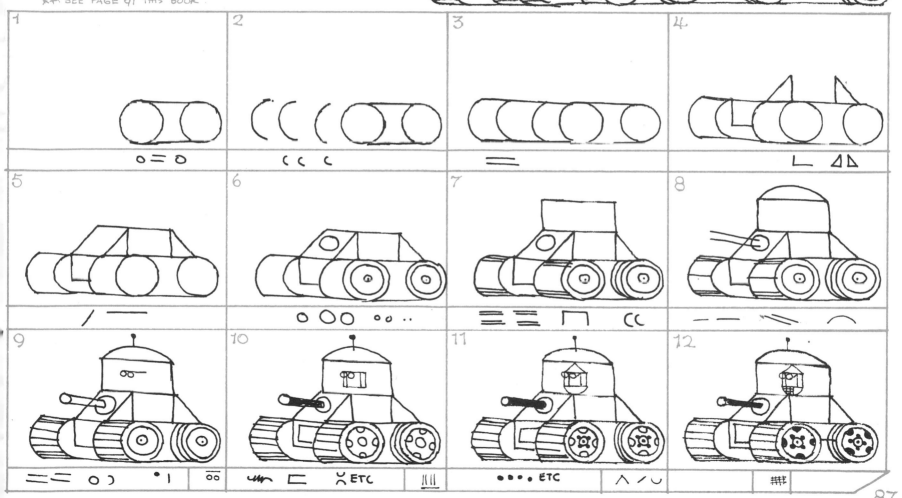

87

A NEEBORT I.C.U. (A FLYING MACHINE)

I.C.U.s LIKE TRAKIRS ARE USED ALONE OR AS
PART OF A LARGER FLYING MACHINE.

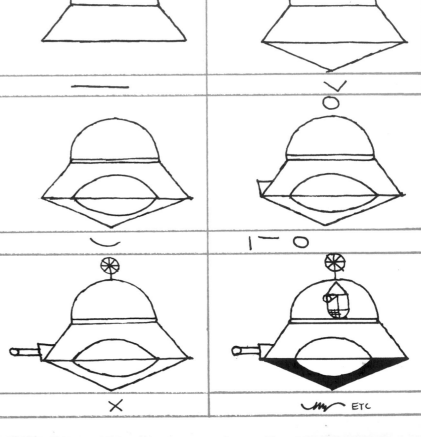

A NEEBORT CARGO CARRIER
USES 4 I.C.U.s ONE ON EACH
CORNER

SIDE VIEW

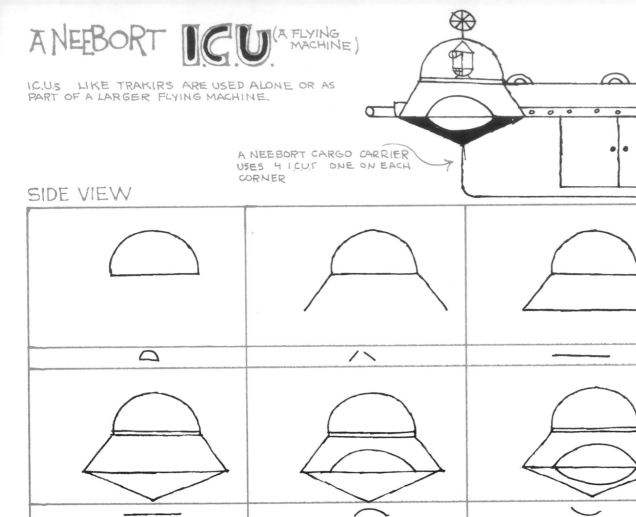

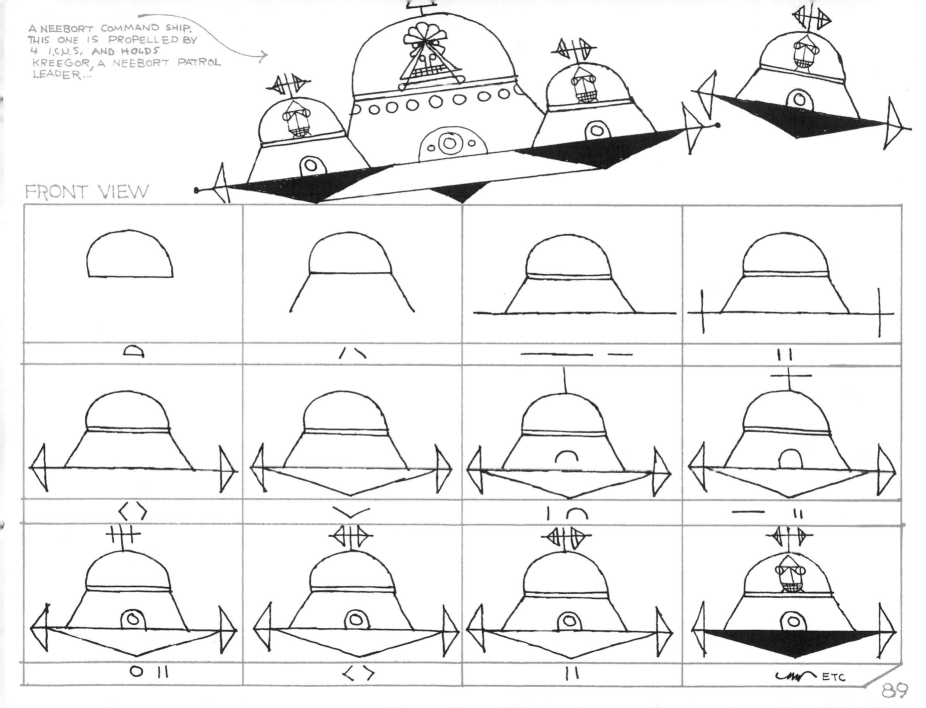

A NEEBORT COMMAND SHIP.
THIS ONE IS PROPELLED BY
4 I.C.U.S, AND HOLDS
KREEGOR, A NEEBORT PATROL
LEADER...

FRONT VIEW

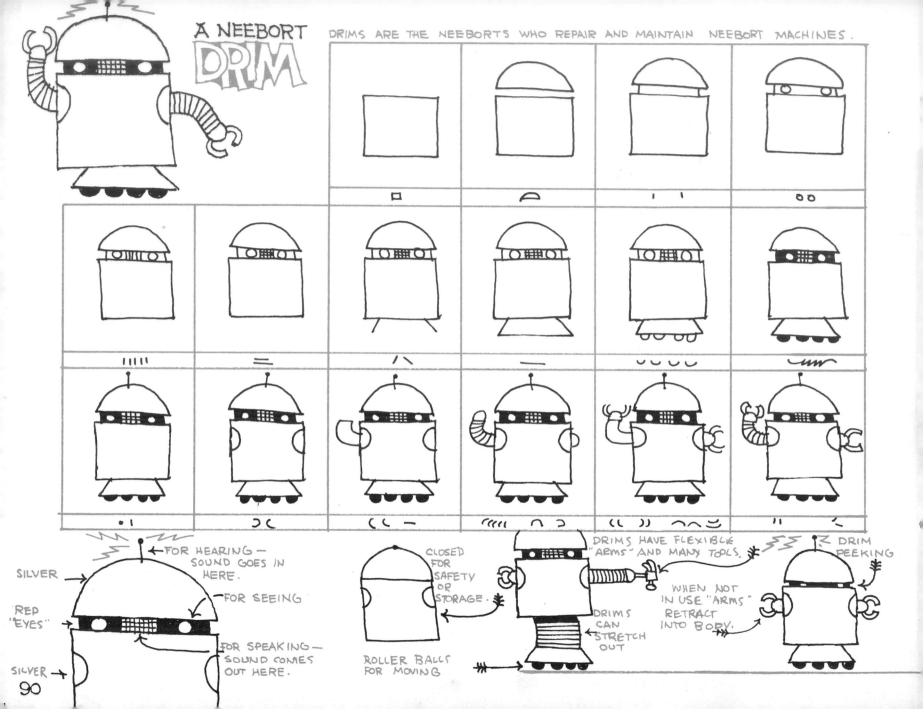

A NEEBORT DRIM

DRIMS ARE THE NEEBORTS WHO REPAIR AND MAINTAIN NEEBORT MACHINES.

FOR HEARING — SOUND GOES IN HERE.

FOR SEEING

FOR SPEAKING — SOUND COMES OUT HERE.

SILVER

REP "EYES"

SILVER

CLOSED FOR SAFETY OR STORAGE.

ROLLER BALLS FOR MOVING

DRIMS CAN STRETCH OUT

DRIMS HAVE FLEXIBLE "ARMS" AND MANY TOOLS.

WHEN NOT IN USE "ARMS" RETRACT INTO BODY.

DRIM PEEKING

GINSFORTWOOZELLFIMMS

GINSFORTWOOZELLFIMMS ARE THE SMALL, PURPLE, FUZZY INHABITANTS OF "FRED" THE SMALLEST OF THE 7 MOONS OF ZORT. (ZORT IS IN THE BIG GREEN DRAWING BOOK.) "FIMMS" HAVE NO BUILDINGS OR MECHANICAL DEVICES. THEY ARE NOMADIC AND SPEND MUCH OF THEIR TIME MOVING FROM PLACE TO PLACE ON THE DARK SIDE OF "FRED"

LOOKING AROUND | ETC | ETC | SIDE VIEW | SOMETIMES | RARE | WINKING | BACK VIEW | TALL | FAT

HUMMING | SAD | GRUMPY | SLEEPY | SLEEPING | KICKING | SITTING | WALKING | RUNNING

ENLARGED VIEW OF A STICKEL.

GINSFORTWOOZELLFIMMS ARE VERY GOOD AT STICKING TOGETHER SINCE EACH STICKEL HAS A LITTLE HOOK ON THE END OF IT. THEY STICK TOGETHER WHEN IN DANGER OR WHEN TRAVELING LONG DISTANCES. THEY TAKE TURNS WALKING, SLEEPING AND HUMMING. THIS FORMATION IS CALLED A FLUMP. IT CAN BE VERY LARGE. THIS IS A SMALL FLUMP.

"FRED"

91

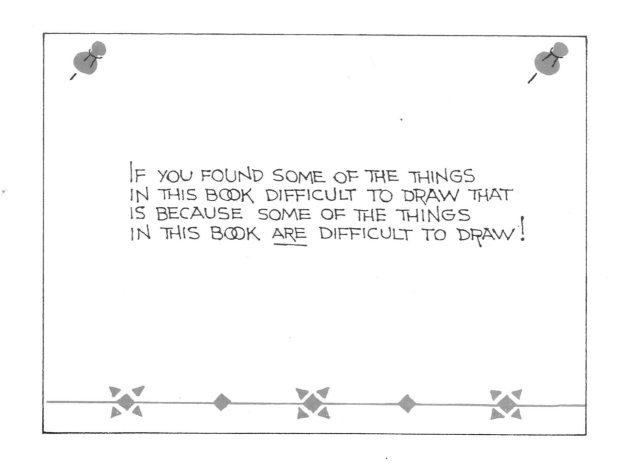

IF YOU FOUND SOME OF THE THINGS
IN THIS BOOK DIFFICULT TO DRAW THAT
IS BECAUSE SOME OF THE THINGS
IN THIS BOOK ARE DIFFICULT TO DRAW!